150 NIFTY TRAVEL GAMES and CARD TRICKS

Written by Kevin Taylor, Joan C. Taylor, K. D. Kuch, and Sheryl Scarborough

Illustrated by Neal Yamamoto

BARNES & NOBLE BOOKS
NEW YORK

This editon published by Barnes & Noble, Inc.,
by arrangement with RGA Publishing Group, Inc.
1996 Barnes & Noble Books

ISBN: 1-56565-461-7

Manufactured in the United States of America

10 9 8 7 6 5 4 3 2 1

CONTENTS

NOTE: The number in the upper right-hand corner of each game or trick indicates the level of difficulty; 1 being the easiest and 3 the hardest.

PLAYER NOTE: If a game or trick needs a certain number of players to work, it is stated under "WHAT YOU'LL NEED." If the number of players is not mentioned, it means the game or activity can be played alone or with any number of people.

"WHAT YOU'LL NEED" NOTE: For most of the card tricks and games all you need is one deck of regular playing cards, the jokers removed, and a table, floor, or flat surface to play on. If a game or trick needs anything more or something different, it is stated under "WHAT YOU'LL NEED."

TRAVEL GAMES

1 GET READY FOR YOUR ADVENTURE!

In this book you'll find all sorts of great activities to enjoy in a car, in a plane, on a train, on a boat, or however you're traveling! But before you leave, here are a few things you'll need to do to prepare for your trip.

WHAT YOU'LL NEED

- shoe box
- foil or wrapping paper
- scissors
- sheet of plain paper
- tape
- markers
- glue
- game supplies for trip
- flat board or lap desk (optional)

BEFORE YOU LEAVE

❶ Flip through the pages of this book. Some of the activities you'll find are things you can do without needing any supplies—word games, sing-alongs, and many more. Others require a few simple supplies, such as pencils, pens, rulers, crayons, scissors, glue, and tape. Collect some of the items for these games and activities *right now!*

❷ Grab your shoe box. Cover the box with foil or wrapping paper by taping it to the box. Do the same with the lid. On a separate piece of paper, write with a marker, "TRAVEL SUPPLIES: PROPERTY OF (your name). DO NOT DISTURB!!" Then, glue this to the side of your travel box. When the box is dry, put all the supplies that you've collected inside.

❸ If you're traveling by car, you may want to bring along a lap desk or a flat board made of wood for a work space. This will make the crafts easier to make and the games easier to play. But remember, with or without a lap desk, never use scissors or other sharp objects when you're zipping along in a moving vehicle. It could be dangerous. So, whenever you see the box below, it means to do your cutting *before* you leave on your trip!

Never use scissors in a moving vehicle, especially a car, bus, or train. Cut out what you need before you leave.

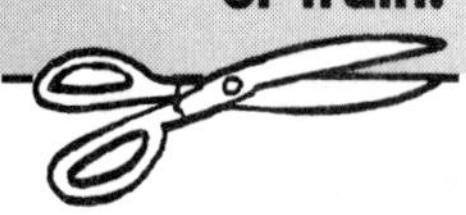

BON VOYAGE!

2 LIVE! FROM THE ROAD

PARENTAL SUPERVISION REQUIRED

Ever wanted to be a reporter and interview all sorts of people? Or do your own weather report or travelogue? Here's your chance to do it all!

WHAT YOU'LL NEED

- portable tape recorder with batteries
- small microphone (optional)
- pencil or pen
- blank cassette tape
- notepad

HOW TO PLAY

1. Grab the tape recorder and put in a blank tape. Most tape recorders have built-in microphones, but you may want to use a small microphone for a clearer sound.

2. Decide exactly what you want to record. Do you want to hold an interview or give a straight newscast? Here are a few ideas:

- Interview your family and friends about the trip.
- Interview people you meet along the way about their trips or home towns.
- Do a newscast from the car, plane, ship, or hotel, reporting on all the most recent happenings on board or in the area.
- Start a diary with dates, times, weather reports, and your observations about the trip.

3. Before you start interviewing anyone, write down a few questions so you'll be prepared. If you are interviewing someone you don't know, stay with a parent at all times. *Never go anywhere alone with a stranger.*

4. When you're finished, play the tape back. If you don't like what you hear, start over! Otherwise, give your recording a name and label it. Don't forget to include the date. Soon, you may have a whole library of your vacations on tape!

ONE STEP FURTHER

Incorporate silly commercials in-between your interviews—be creative!

3 TRUNKS, EARS, AND TAILS

Can't decide who gets the front seat? The window seat? The last soda? Here's a surefire and fun way to settle all your traveling disputes. It makes a good game, too.

WHAT YOU'LL NEED

• two or more players

HOW TO PLAY

1. The next time you and your brother or sister can't stop bickering, look at each other, shake hands, and say, "Trunks, Ears, and Tails."

2. Then both of you make a fist, pound it into your other hand once as you both say "Trunks." Pound your fists again and say "Ears," and pound your fists a third time as you both say "Tails."

3. On the third pound (the "Tails" pound), each of you does one of three things:

- Put out your index finger, meaning "Trunk," (which stands for the trunk on an elephant).
- Put out your index finger and your middle finger, meaning "Ears," (which stands for a cat's ears).
- Put out your pinky finger, meaning "Tail," (which stands for a mouse's tail).

4. How do you decide the winner? Easy! The elephant can step on the cat, so the elephant wins out over the cat. The cat can catch the mouse, so the cat wins out over the mouse. And since mice can spook elephants, the mouse wins out over the elephant!

ROCKY MOUNTAIN TREASURE TUMBLE

Make it down the mountain with your hidden treasure—but don't fall off the edge, or you'll lose both your riches and the game!

WHAT YOU'LL NEED

- cardboard
- ruler
- scissors
- pens, pencils, markers, or crayons
- seven bobby pins
- tape
- penny

Never use scissors in a moving vehicle, especially a car, bus, or train. Cut out what you need before you leave.

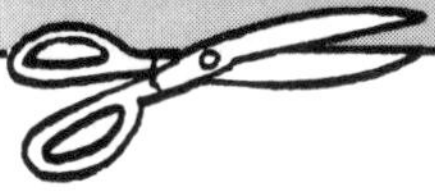

BEFORE YOU LEAVE

Use a ruler to cut the cardboard to playing size, which is 6 by 11 inches. Now you're ready to prepare the game board, which can be done before you leave or while traveling.

PREPARING YOUR GAME BOARD

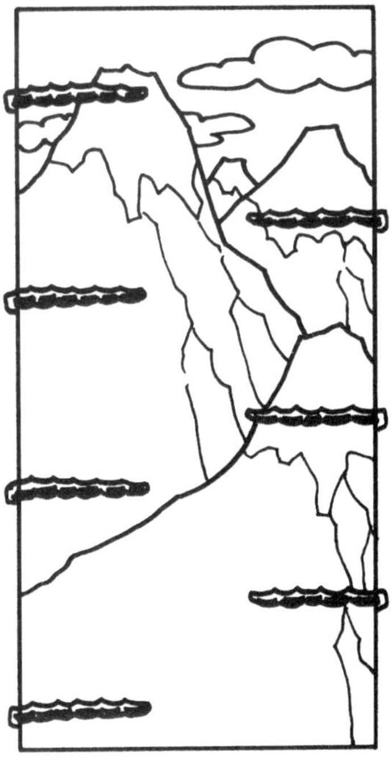

1. Make sure your cardboard is in a vertical position. Then draw a huge mountain on the cardboard piece using pens, pencils, markers, or crayons.

2. Now clip your bobby pins onto the cardboard in the positions shown. The ridged side of the bobby pins should be on the front of the game board. With tape, secure the bobby pins to the back of the cardboard. These will be your "footholds" for your challenging mountain descent.

3. Draw a flag and write "Start" above the top left bobby pin. Then draw a small house with the word "Home" above the bottom left bobby pin. Finally, draw a treasure chest above each of the

rest of the bobby pins, close to the edge of the cardboard. Write the number 10 inside each treasure chest and inside the house.

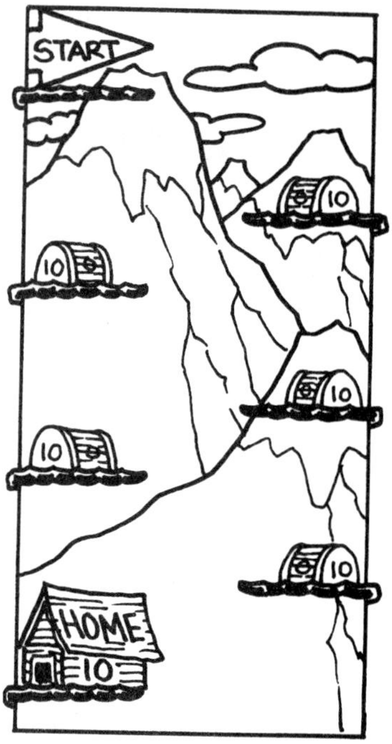

HOW TO PLAY

1. Now that your game board is complete, place a penny at "Start" and turn on your imagination. That penny is you, and your goal is to reach "Home" and pick up as many treasure points as you can along the way.

2. Pick your way down the treacherous path by gently tilting the board from side to side. You will drop to the next foothold. There you will discover a hidden treasure. Each time you safely make it (by covering each treasure with your penny), you receive 10 points.

3. If you fall off the mountain (the game board), you must start back up at the top. You lose all the treasure points you've earned, along with an additional minus 10 points. The player with the most treasure points at the end of three turns wins.

ONE STEP FURTHER

Add a monster to the game! Draw Bigfoot—the horrible, hairy monster of the Rockies—on your game board, and if your penny touches him, you automatically lose!

5 7-11 ZIP! ZAP!

Here's a game that will challenge your mind and twist your tongue. And remember—don't zip when you should zap!

WHAT YOU'LL NEED

- two or more players

HOW TO PLAY

❶ Get ready for fast action! To begin playing, every player takes a turn counting, beginning with the number 1 ("1-2-3" etc.). Easy, right? Here's the tricky part: When the count reaches 7, a multiple of 7 (like 14 or 28), or a number with 7 in it (like 17 or 27), the person whose turn it is has to say "zip!" instead of the number.

❷ To make things even more challenging, when the count reaches 11 or a multiple of 11 (like 22 or 33), the person whose turn it is says "zap!" instead.

❸ Ready for a practice? "1-2-3-4-5-6-zip!-8-9-10-zap!-12-13-zip!-15-16-zip!-18-19-20-zip!-zap!" And so on. Make sure everybody gets his or her turn—no skipping. Got it? Good!

❹ If you make a mistake on the number or on a "zip!" or a "zap!," you're out. The last one in wins. Now see how fast and how high you can count!

6 VACATION CONCENTRATION

Are you "game" for a competition that will test your memory and concentration skills? Then get playing!

WHAT YOU'LL NEED

- two or more players
- two shoe box tops
- ruler
- pen or pencil
- scissors

Never use scissors in a moving vehicle, especially a car, bus, or train. Cut out what you need before you leave.

BEFORE YOU LEAVE

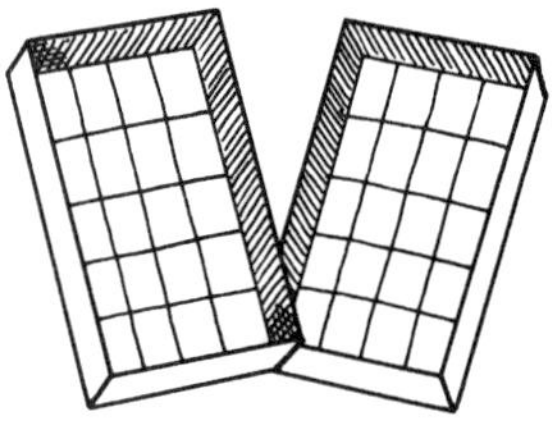

1. With a ruler, divide each shoe box top equally into 20 squares (three lines long ways, four lines across).

2. Trim off the edges of one shoe box top, then cut along the lines to create 20 game pieces. The second shoe box top is your game board.

3. Write an "A" on two pieces, a "B" on two pieces, a "C" on two pieces, and so on down to "J." (You can write the letters while you're traveling if you want to.)

HOW TO PLAY

1. Turn the pieces facedown and mix them up. Place each piece facedown on the game board.

2. Taking turns, flip over two pieces and look for a match. Keep the ones you match.

3. The player with the most pairs at the end wins! A tie? Play again!

7 "AND WHATCHA GONNA BRING?"

This alphabet game is especially fun with a large group. Once you get the hang of it, it's as easy as A-B-C!

WHAT YOU'LL NEED

- two or more players

HOW TO PLAY

1. To begin, the first player says, "I'm going on down to the park." The other players respond, "And whatcha gonna bring?" The first player answers back, "I'm going on down to the park and I'm bringing an alligator" (or anything else that begins with the letter "A").

2. Then the second player says, "I'm going on down to the park." The others ask, "And whatcha gonna bring?" The second player must repeat the "A" word, and then think of a "B" word. For example, the player might say: "I'm going on down to the park and I'm bringing an alligator and a baby" (or a baseball, bear, or banana).

3. Then the next player takes his or her turn, repeating all the things that have gone before and naming something that begins with "C." Continue taking turns coming up with a word that begins with the next letter in the alphabet. If you can't remember all the things that went before, get them out of order, or can't think of a word that begins with the correct letter, then—you guessed it—you're out! And no fair writing the words down. This is a test of your memory! The last person in is the winner.

8

T-SHIRT TRAVELOGUE

2

PARENTAL SUPERVISION REQUIRED

Have you ever wished you could break your leg just so you could get all your friends to sign your cast? Instead, have everyone you meet on your trip sign your shirt. You'll meet lots of new friends, and what's more, there's no pain involved!

WHAT YOU'LL NEED

- old white T-shirt
- permanent pens or markers, various colors

HOW TO PLAY

1. First of all, choose a large T-shirt that your parents won't mind you marking up.

2. Then, wherever you go on your trip, get everyone you meet to sign your shirt with his or her name and a message, using the permanent pen or marker. Ask food servers, hotel managers, tour guides, gas station attendants—anyone! When asking people to sign your shirt, stay with a parent at all times. *Never go anywhere alone with a stranger.*

3. Give each person a different color marker to make your shirt as colorful as possible.

ONE STEP FURTHER

For an extra twist and even nuttier memories, find only people whose names start with the same letter as the place you're visiting, such as "Andy from Anchorage" or "Beth from Berthoud."

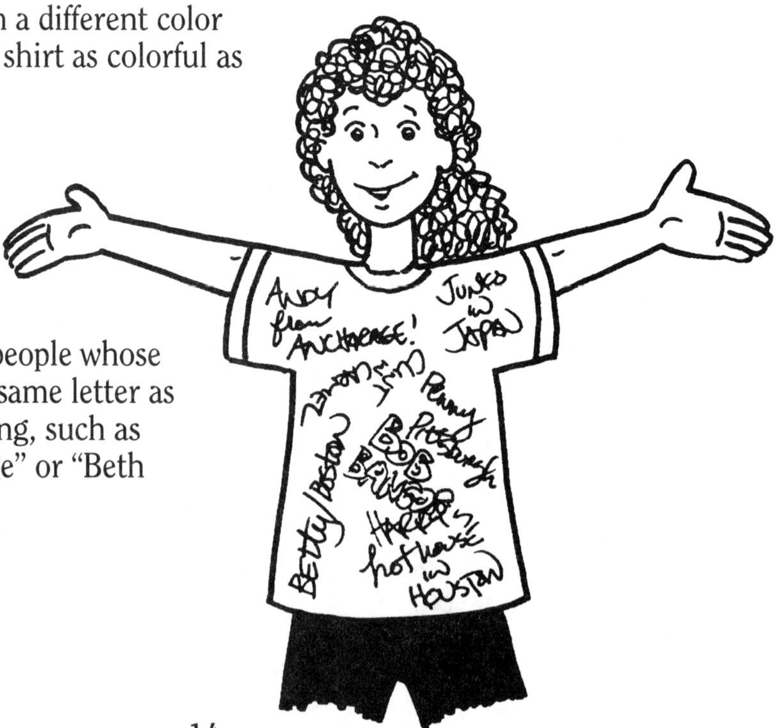

9 BLINDFOLD DRAWING

Here's your chance to see what kind of silly pictures you can make in this hilarious game where your ears and your hand are the only "eyes" you have!

WHAT YOU'LL NEED

- two or more players
- paper
- pen or pencil
- hard surface (optional)
- scarf, bandanna, or sock

HOW TO PLAY

1. Each player needs a piece of paper and a pen or pencil. If possible, put the paper on a hard surface.

2. All players except for one should tie a blindfold (the scarf, bandanna, or sock) around their heads so they can't see anything. Now the one unblindfolded player should describe the passing scenery as accurately as possible. The "blind" players need to listen carefully and draw what is being described. No fair peeking!

3. Compare drawings. Whose picture looks the most like the scenery you've passed? Whose looks most like a bunch of shapeless blobs? Let Mom or Dad be the judge!

4. Play until every player has had a chance to describe the scenery.

10 VACATION AVIATION

Create super paper jets that you design and build while you're traveling, then test them at different stops along the way. See who builds the plane that flies the farthest, straightest, longest—and has the fewest collisions!

WHAT YOU'LL NEED

- paper
- pen or pencil
- colored markers (optional)
- ruler
- watch with a second hand

HOW TO PLAY

1 First, create and build your very own paper airplane—make it as simple or as fancy as you want! With colored markers, draw designs such as flames or shooting stars on the sides and nose. Don't forget to give each plane a name.

2 Make up a chart like the one pictured here. Remember to include statistics such as the flight number, plane name, date and time, weather conditions, flight distance, flight time (use a watch with a second hand), and any other important information.

3 Now you're all set for the great plane race! Once your mom or dad stops the car (don't throw the planes in the car—they may never fly again if your parents get a hold of them!), everyone flies his or her plane and records the statistics on the chart. The plane that flies the furthest and for the longest amount of time wins! Don't just stop with one flight. Fly the planes several times to see which plane is the day's top flyer.

FLIGHT NUMBER	PLANE NAME	DATE/TIME	WEATHER CONDITIONS	FLIGHT DISTANCE	FLIGHT TIME
1	SPARK PLUG	JUNE 2 9:20 AM	COLD, WINDY	20 FEET	17 SECONDS
2	SPARK PLUG	JUNE 2 9:22 AM	COLD, WINDY	19 FEET	15 SECONDS
1	SOPWITH CAMEL	JUNE 2 9:25 AM	COLD, WINDY	14 FEET	10 SECONDS
2	SOPWITH CAMEL	JUNE 2 9:28 AM	COLD, WINDY	17 FEET	13 SECONDS
1	RED BARON	JUNE 2 12 NOON	WARM, LIGHT BREEZE	20 FEET	16 SECONDS
3	SPARK PLUG	JUNE 2 12:02 PM	WARM, LIGHT BREEZE	18 FEET	14 SECO
1	PAPPY BOYNTON	JUNE 2 12:05 PM	WARM, LIGHT BREEZE	17 FEET	[illegible]

11 BIG ADVENTURE MINI-BOOK

This is a perfect way to record your trip! Create your own travel journal using paper, string, and your imagination.

WHAT YOU'LL NEED

- 10 to 20 sheets of 8½-by-11-inch paper
- hole puncher
- string, three pieces about 6 inches long
- scissors
- pens or pencils
- glue
- tape
- postcards, leaves, napkins, and anything you find on your trip that you want to include

Never use scissors in a moving vehicle, especially a car, bus, or train. Cut out what you need before you leave.

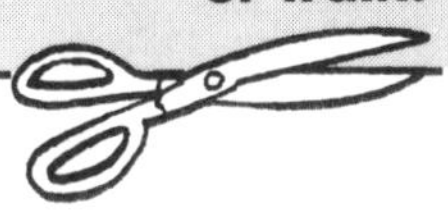

BEFORE YOU LEAVE

❶ You'll want to get your book put together before you leave in case something interesting happens the moment your trip begins! To start, fold each sheet of paper in half, horizontally. Lay the open sheets on top of each other, then fold them all together so that the folds are on the left side.

❷ When you've got the sheets lined up, punch three holes along the left side, about ½ inch from the folded edge. You've got the beginnings of your travel book!

❸ Now thread a piece of string through each of the holes and tie it carefully. Be gentle—make sure the paper doesn't get wrinkled or torn.

HOW TO PLAY

Now you're ready to fill the book with travel mementos—anything you want to remember! Collect autographs, draw pictures of the places you visit, and write about funny things that happen on the trip. Also, tape or glue souvenirs in your book, such as napkins from restaurants, postcards, or unusual leaves from your favorite campgrounds or parks. Don't forget to label each page with the date and location. When you get home, you'll have a book full of memories—a terrific tale of your Big Adventure Vacation!

12 MAGICAL MYSTERY PICTURES

Make your own magnificent work of art! How about a purple sun or orange grass? Even a neon green castle! You'll be amazed at your own creations!

WHAT YOU'LL NEED

- paper
- pen or pencil
- crayons
- hard surface
- paper clip or coin

HOW TO PLAY

❶ Draw an abstract design on a piece of paper.

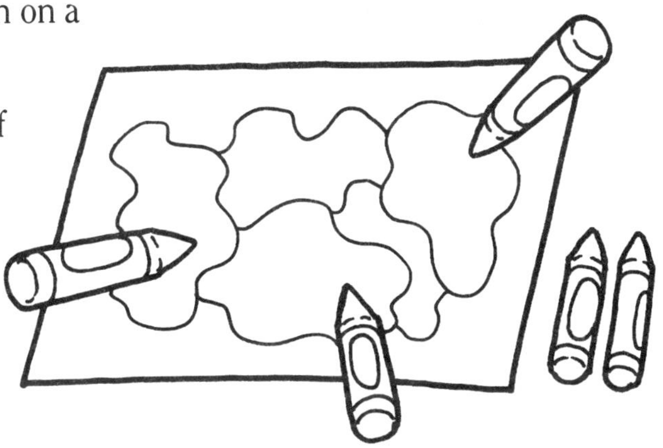

❷ Color in all the parts of your design, using as many color crayons as you can. It is important to press down hard with your crayons, so find a sturdy surface to work on.

❸ Now completely cover the colorful design with black crayon. Rub really hard so you can't see *any* other color peeking through!

❹ Using an unfolded paper clip or the side of a coin, scratch out the picture of your choice by scraping off the black crayon. You can draw a picture of your pet or your family, or you may want to write your name in big block letters. Because you don't know the colors underneath the black crayon, you will be surprised by what appears. One note of caution: This game may result in black crayon smudges on the sides of your hands. Don't smear them on your face!

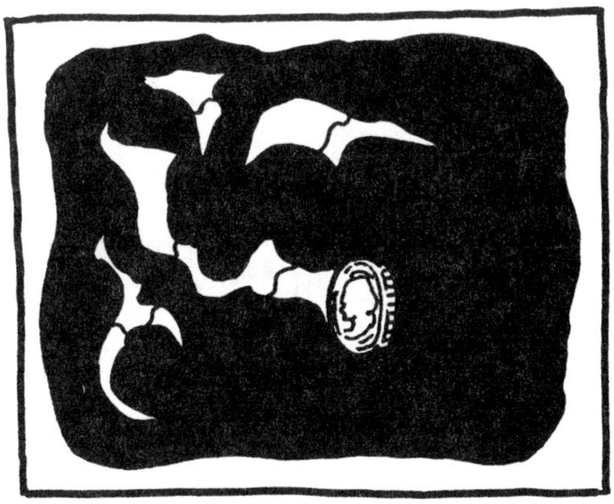

13

LICENSE TO SPELL

This spelling game based on the license plates of passing cars definitely "spells" hours of fun for you and your traveling buddies.

WHAT YOU'LL NEED

- three or more players
- paper
- pens or pencils
- passing cars

HOW TO PLAY

1 All the players decide on a subject, such as "Movies." Other category ideas include science fiction books, sports stars, cars, monsters, cartoon characters, dinosaurs, superheroes, and wild animals.

2 Choose one player to be the "caller." You can rotate who the caller is every round or change callers every game.

3 Ask the caller to call out all the letters from the license plate numbers of passing cars. Everybody else writes them down.

4 The first player to spell the name of a title or object within the subject, using only the letters called out from the licence plates, wins the round. The winner gets a point for each letter used. You can use each letter only once. If two people come up with a word at the same time, whoever has the longest word (has used the most letters) wins that round. A game can be made up of anywhere from five to ten rounds or more!

14 A-MAZE-ING PORTABLE PINBALL

You'll find out who has got the quickest reflexes and sharpest eye with this great travel maze game that you design, build, and play yourself!

WHAT YOU'LL NEED

- shoe box top (use the one from your supply box)
- heavy cardboard (like the flaps from a packing box)
- 8½-by-11-inch construction paper
- scissors
- cotton balls
- glue
- pen or pencil
- paper clips
- marbles

Never use scissors in a moving vehicle, especially a car, bus, or train. Cut out what you need before you leave.

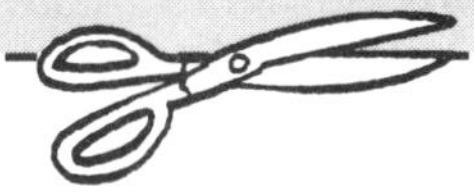

BEFORE YOU LEAVE

❶ Cut the piece of cardboard to fit snugly inside the shoe box top. This will be your game board. When you're ready to play the game, slip this piece of cardboard into your supply box lid.

❷ Cut the paper into four or five different sizes of rectangles, no bigger than 8 inches long.

PREPARING YOUR GAME BOARD

❶ The object of this game is to get your marble through the maze game board that you create yourself. In your maze, you will create tunnels and arches that you must successfully go through, as well as bottomless holes and sandpits that you must avoid. Begin with your "Start" and "Finish." To make the "Start," roll a cut-out rectangle into a cylinder tunnel (it must be wide enough for your marble to fit through), glue the edges together, then glue it into the bottom right-hand corner of your game board. Next to this first tunnel, write "Start."

❷ For the "Finish," unbend three paper clips so you have three arches, then poke the ends into the game board in the bottom left-hand corner. Poke them all the way through the cardboard and bend the ends against the back of the cardboard so they stay secure. At the end of the row of arches write "Finish." Draw a curvy line that travels around your game board, beginning at "Start" and ending at "Finish." This will be the path of your maze.

❸ With your pen or pencil, poke four or five holes into your game board alongside the path you just drew, just a bit to one side or the other. Space them out all along the path. Wiggle your finger inside each hole to make them big enough to catch a marble temporarily, but not so big that the marble falls all the way in! These will be your "bottomless holes."

❹ Make one or two more cylinder tunnels and glue the ends together, then glue them onto different places along your path. Using several more paper clips, build a few more arches along your path. It doesn't matter where the tunnels and arches are placed—you can make your maze as easy or as difficult as you want.

❺ Spread two or three small spots of glue off to the sides of your path, and place a little cotton on top of these spots. These will be your "sandpits," and they must be avoided at all costs!

HOW TO PLAY

Now you're ready to play! The edges of the shoe box top will keep your marble on the board. Each arch and tunnel are worth two points, and the sandpits and bottomless holes are minus two points. Place a marble at "Start" and tilt the game board back and forth, trying to stay on the path while scoring points and avoiding the sandpits. When you reach "Finish," add up all your points. The player with the most points wins!

17 POSTCARD PASSION 2

Take a few minutes to tell your friends and family back home how much you miss them with your personalized postcards!

WHAT YOU'LL NEED

- large piece of poster board
- ruler (optional)
- scissors
- colorful markers
- several postcard stamps
- pen
- camera (optional)
- glue (optional)

Never use scissors in a moving vehicle, especially a car, bus, or train. Cut out what you need before you leave.

BEFORE YOU LEAVE

Cut the poster board into several rectangles 4¼ by 6 inches. These will be your postcards.

HOW TO PLAY

❶ On your trip, look for memorable places or landmarks that you can draw. When you see something worth remembering, draw a picture of it.

❷ Then, at your next destination, write a note, pop a stamp on it, address it, and send it to a buddy. It's that easy!

❸ If you can, take photos of the places you visit. Then when you stay over somewhere, take the film to an hour-developing shop. Once you get your photos back, glue them to the fronts of the postcards. Don't forget to add a personal note!

18 MOBILE PHONE

Who needs an expensive portable phone when you can play this great "telephone" game—and all you need are your buddies and some good gossip!

WHAT YOU'LL NEED

- four or more players
- pen or pencil
- paper

HOW TO PLAY

❶ To start, one player writes a story that is three to six sentences long. The story must include one person, one place, and one thing that he or she has seen on the trip. Outside of that, the story can be about anything! The player must keep this story a secret!

❷ The first player then leans over to the next player and whispers the story into his or her ear. You're only allowed to whisper the story *one* time, so whisper clearly and slowly!

❸ The next player then whispers the story to the next player, and so on until the last player has heard it. Then the last player says the story out loud. Compare it to the story that was written down, and you'll all be surprised at how much it has changed! (Now you know how rumors start at school!)

19 PUZZLE CARDS

Here's a cool card game that's as much fun to make as it is to play. Create your own deck of cards with pictures from old magazines and see which player can find the pieces and put together the most puzzles!

WHAT YOU'LL NEED

- two to four players
- old magazines
- 16 pieces of cardboard or other heavy paper, $8\frac{1}{2}$ by 11 inches each
- scissors
- glue

Never use scissors in a moving vehicle, especially a car, bus, or train. Cut out what you need before you leave.

BEFORE YOU LEAVE

1. Go through some old magazines, choosing pictures that fill a full page. You need at least 15 or 16 full-page pictures, so if you have four players, each should find four pictures; if you have three players, each should find five; and if you have only two players, each will need to find eight!

2. Carefully cut or tear the pictures out of the magazines and glue them onto the pieces of cardboard or heavy paper.

3. Cut each picture into four equal pieces. You should end up with 60 or 64 cards.

HOW TO PLAY

1 Choose one player to be the dealer. The dealer collects all the cards and shuffles them. Each player is dealt seven cards, and should go through his or her cards and group together any cards that are parts of the same picture.

2 The dealer then puts the remaining cards facedown, and turns over the top card and places it next to the deck.

3 Going in a circle, each player chooses to take either the faceup card or a new one from the deck. Then that player discards one card from his or her hand onto the faceup pile.

4 Around and around it goes. Anytime players complete a puzzle by collecting all four of the cards from one picture, they place those cards in a separate pile and draw four new cards from the facedown deck.

5 When all the cards are gone from the facedown deck, reshuffle all the cards from the faceup pile (except the top one), place them facedown, and keep playing. Here's how to determine a winner:

(two players): the first player to make five complete puzzles
(three players): the first player to make four complete puzzles
(four players): the first player to make three complete puzzles

Now play again! Or, think of another game to play with your new deck of cards!

20 LEAVE 'EM LAUGHING

1

Who can keep the straightest face? Find out in this sidesplitting game where the object is to make the other players laugh without cracking up yourself! Good luck, and may the biggest clown win!

WHAT YOU'LL NEED

- two or more players
- paper
- pencil

HOW TO PLAY

1. The first player gets 30 seconds to do the silliest thing he or she can think of to try to make the others laugh: sing the alphabet in a crazy way, yodel nursery rhymes, or make goofy faces. Players get one point for each player they make laugh, and lose one for each time they laugh at themselves or someone else.

2. Appoint one person to keep track of the score on a piece of paper. The scorekeeper can play the game, too. When it's his or her turn to make others laugh, someone else can keep score that round.

3. Each player takes a turn to try to get everyone else to crack a giggle. The first person to reach 10 points wins!

ONE STEP FURTHER

This is also a great game to play throughout the day. Before you leave, everyone in the car agrees that at any moment one of the players might spring a surprise-attack crazy act on the others. Each person can keep track of his or her points.

21 THE ROADSIDE SCRAMBLER

Did you ever stop to think about how many different words you can make from the letters "vacation"? "Can," "tin," "not"—how about "action"? Now the race is on to see how many words you can make from the cities, streets, and signs you see along the way!

WHAT YOU'LL NEED

- two or more players
- paper
- pen or pencil
- timer or watch with second hand

HOW TO PLAY

❶ Pick someone to be the caller. (The caller can also play the game.) The caller calls out the first two words from the first sign he or she sees.

❷ The players write these two words down, and the race is on. Use the letters in the words to form as many new words as you can. For example, if the first sign the caller sees reads, "Loveland, Colorado: Next Exit," the caller announces "Loveland, Colorado." The players write down "Loveland, Colorado," and try to form smaller, new words, such as "road," "cove," "cave," "doodle," and others. Each letter in each word equals one point.

❸ After two minutes, the caller calls time. Everyone now adds up his or her points. The player with the most points wins!

22 CARTOON FLIP BOOK

Here's how to create your own cartoon characters having their own zany adventures. Who knows—maybe *your* cartoon character will have its own Saturday morning TV show one day.

WHAT YOU'LL NEED

- pens or pencils
- old, thick paperback book that your parents don't want (no library or school books!) or a pad of Post-It™ notes

HOW TO PLAY

1. Think of a really silly character and a series of actions he or she (or it!) can do. Keep it simple at first—you may even want to do this activity using only stick figures.

2. In the bottom right corner of the first page of the paperback or the first Post-It™ note, draw the first scene of your character doing something silly, like slipping on a banana peel, doing a handstand on the stairs, skateboarding wildly, or chasing a cow around a tree.

3. On each of the following right-hand pages, draw the same picture—almost! Each time you draw it, change it just a little bit, adding a little movement. For example, if your monkey man is slipping on a banana peel, on the next page you may have his hat start to fall off. On each page, the hat should get closer and closer to the ground. Keep adding to your "cartoon" until all the pages are filled or your character's action is complete. The blank pages in the book or notepad can be filled up later with additional cartoons.

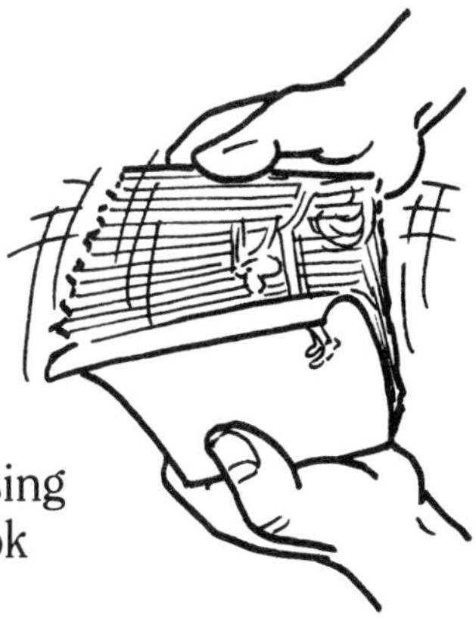

4. Now you're ready for the show. Flip through your "cartoon" quickly, trying not to skip pages as you go. Watch your character run, jump, or fly through the air!

ONE STEP FURTHER

Once you've completed one cartoon, do it again, using the *top* corner of the pages. And then, turn the book over and araw on the other sides of the pages.

23 EVERYBODY'S GOT A STORY

This never-ending story will provide never-ending fun for a long trip.

WHAT YOU'LL NEED

- two or more players
- blank tape
- tape recorder with batteries
- stop watch or watch

HOW TO PLAY

1. One player begins the story with a single line, such as: "Once upon a time, there lived a lonely bubble gum collector." Each player then takes a turn adding one line to the story. There's just one catch—each player has to start his or her first line with the last word from the line before! So a story might go like this:

   Player #1: "Once upon a time, there lived a lonely bubble gum collector…"
   Player #2: "Collector Curt he was called, and he loved gum, especially peanut…"
   Player #3: "Peanut butter gum and bananas were Curt's favorite breakfast…"

2. Once everyone has had a turn, go back to the first player. Go around the group for a designated amount of time. (Usually three to five minutes works well.)

3. Be sure to try tape recording your story—you'll get a laugh every time you hear it!

24 SENSATIONALLY SILLY STORIES

Test your creative writing skills by making up crazy stories with words you tear out of a magazine. See what kinds of tall tales you and your friends or siblings can come up with—but no fair trading words.

WHAT YOU'LL NEED

- some old magazines
- glue stick
- large sheets of paper (one per player)

HOW TO PLAY

1 Carefully tear out 50 words from a magazine and lay them out on a sheet of paper. Find at least one word beginning with each letter of the alphabet.

2 Arrange the words to make a short story. You don't have to use all of the words. Then, once you've laid the words out in the order you want, glue them down to the sheet of paper. This way, a nasty bump in the road won't send your story flying!

3 Read your stories out loud to each other. The most clever one wins (all participants can vote to decide the winner).

ONE STEP FURTHER

Try this game with teams—one team tears out 50 words for the other team and vice versa. Who can write the best (or most ridiculous) story? Have a parent judge. Tiebreakers can be decided based on which team was able to incorporate the most words into the story.

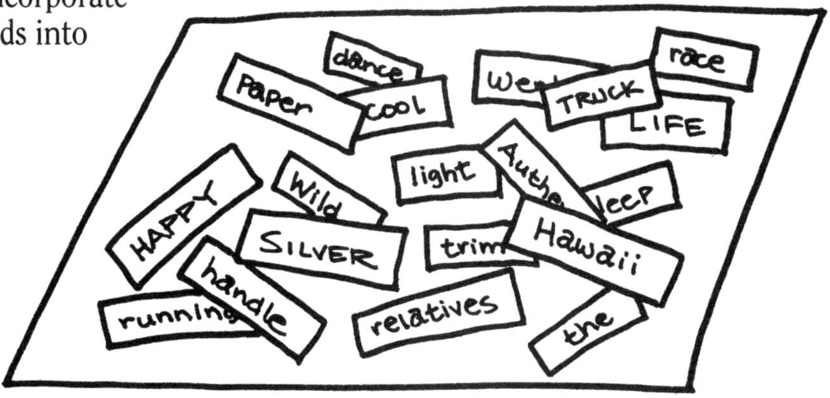

25 WORD RACERS!

Can you find the hidden words? Do you think you could hide words so that no one else can find them? Here's your chance to find out in this do-it-yourself puzzle. You determine how hard it will be to solve!

WHAT YOU'LL NEED

- two or more players
- scratch paper
- pen or pencil
- 8½-by-11-inch graph paper or 8½-by-11-inch plain paper and ruler (one per player)

HOW TO PLAY

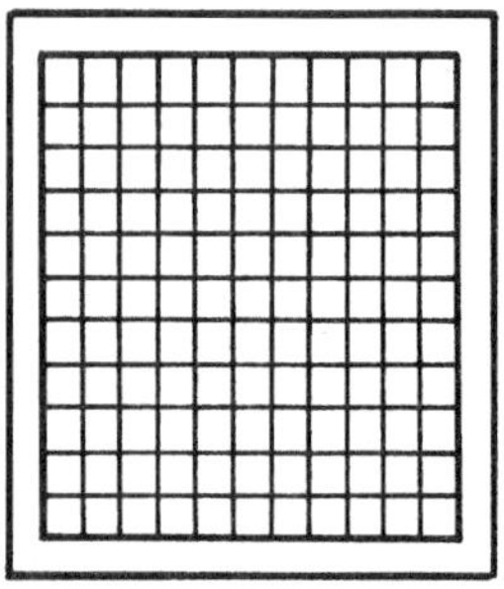

❶ Each player decides on his or her own secret subject, then chooses 10 words that are based on that subject (such as 10 kinds of animals, 10 flavors of ice cream, and 10 places to visit). Write them down on scratch paper, and don't show anyone!

❷ If you have graph paper, skip to the next step; otherwise, draw a big square on your sheet of 8½-by-11-inch plain paper. Then draw 12 lines going up and down and 12 lines going across, with about ½-inch space between each line. Make the lines as straight as you can, using a ruler if you have one. Now you have 121 boxes.

❸ Write each of your 10 words in connecting boxes (one letter in each box). Your words can go upward, downward, backward, forward, or even diagonally! Around all your words, write extra random letters so your original words are lost in a word puzzle. Then circle one of your hidden words as a hint about your subject.

❹ All the players trade puzzles, and the race is on! The first one to find all the hidden words and guess the subject wins.

26 SON OF HANGMAN

Here's a new twist on an old favorite!

WHAT YOU'LL NEED

- two or more players
- paper
- pen or pencil

HOW TO PLAY

1 One player thinks of a phrase, famous saying, well-known name, or the title of a book or movie. On a piece of paper, the player then draws the same number of lines as there are letters in the phrase, just like Hangman or the TV show "Wheel of Fortune." Make sure to leave a space between each word. For example, if the phrase is "A fish out of water," the player would draw lines like this:

–   – – – –   – – –   – –   – – – – –

2 Then, the player also thinks of a picture to draw that will give clues to the answer of the puzzle. The picture should have eight objects in it, and *no more than* eight. Using the phrase above, the player might decide to draw a picture of a dead-looking fish lying on a beach away from the water. The fish would be one object, the fish's eye another, the waves another, and so on.

3 Now the game begins! The second player tries to solve the puzzle by guessing letters one at a time that are in the phrase. If the second player guesses correctly, the first player writes that letter in the correct place in the phrase. If the guess is incorrect, the first player draws one object of the picture. For example, let's say that after 10 turns, the second player has guessed "A - E - I - O - U - T - C - B - W - J." That's seven correct letters and three incorrect letters. The game now looks like this:

A _I__ OUT O_ WATE_

4 The first player has drawn three objects of the picture, one for each miss. If the first player completes the picture before the second player guesses the phrase, the first player wins. But, if the second player guesses the phrase correctly first, he or she wins!

5 Get it? Good! Then switch places so everyone gets a chance to guess and create a puzzle.

27 GET OFF MY BACK!

1

You'll have hours of back-to-back fun when you play this unique spelling and guessing game where you use each other's back as a blackboard. But beware: This game is not for the ticklish!

WHAT YOU'LL NEED

- two players
- paper
- pen or pencil

HOW TO PLAY

1. Each player chooses a category, such as types of birds, words that start with "B," or parts of the body. Keep the category pretty simple, and *keep it to yourself!*

2. Think of five things that would be included in your category. For types of birds, it might be sparrow, crow, blue jay, turkey, and eagle. You may want to write down your five objects on paper so you don't forget any!

3. Once both players have figured out their categories and words, one player traces the first word, letter by letter, on the other player's back with his or her index finger. Pause a moment between each letter. You're only allowed to draw each letter in the word once, so go slowly and write big.

4. Once the player has completed the word, the second player tries to figure it out, but keeps quiet about his or her guess (the second player can write it down if he or she wants to). The second player then turns around and writes a word from his or her chosen category on the back of the first player.

5. Continue playing until both players have written all the words in the category on the other's back.

6. Whoever figures out the category first wins. If neither player can figure out the category, or if both players figure it out at the same time, it's a tie, so play again. (In fact, even if it's not a tie, why not play again?)

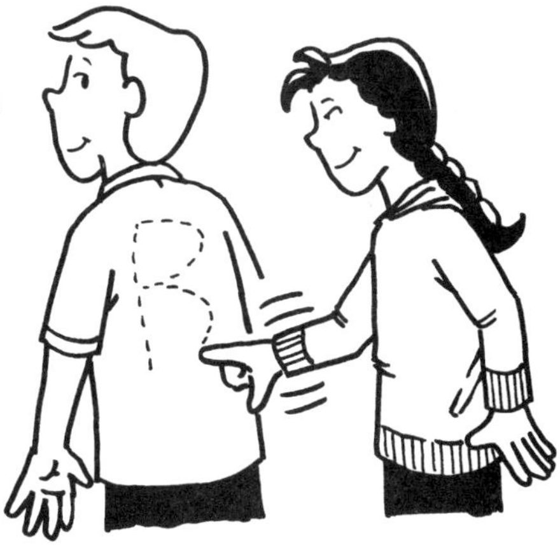

28 THE NAME GAME

Here's a terrific name game in which you have to pay close attention to all of the questions and all of the answers. Put all the clues together and see if you can guess who your mystery person is!

WHAT YOU'LL NEED

- two or more players
- a pen or pencil
- 3-by-5-inch index cards

HOW TO PLAY

1. Each player writes down five famous names, each one on a separate index card. Famous names work the best, but they don't have to be real—try characters from cartoons or books.

2. Everyone draws one name from the person on his or her left, but *without looking* at it!

3. The players then hold the name they chose up to their foreheads so all the other players can see the name they picked.

4. Going around in a circle, each player takes a turn asking one question about the name he or she selected. Only yes or no questions are allowed. Examples: "Is the person a man?" "Is the person make-believe?" "Does this person wear a cape?"

5. Keep asking questions that are more and more exact to narrow down your person's identity. When you think you've got the answer, announce your identity. But be careful—two wrong guesses and you're out!

6. The first player to guess correctly wins. Keep playing until all the names are used up. Then write some more and start again!

29 FIVE IN A LINE

Are you bored with tic-tac-toe? This game is much more challenging, and you can play it with up to four (or even more!) players.

WHAT YOU'LL NEED

- two or more players
- pen or pencil
- 8½-by-11-inch graph paper or 8½-by-11-inch plain paper and ruler

HOW TO PLAY

❶ First, you need to draw your game board. On a piece of paper, draw a large box. Inside the box, use a ruler to draw lines running vertically and horizontally, each line about ½ inch from the other. You'll end up with a game board made up of a box with a few hundred squares. If you have graph paper, you can use the squares already printed.

❷ The object of the game is to be the first player to get "five in a line." It's played a little like tic-tac-toe, but it's on a much bigger board and you need to get *five* in a row—up and down, across, or diagonally. Also, you can play with more than two players.

❸ The rules are simple, but the strategy is complicated, so stay alert! After you decide who goes first, players take turns writing the first letter of their first name in any square, one square per turn, trying to be the first to get five initials in a row. If two of the players have the same initial, one of the players should use the first and second letters of his or her first name. Be sure to watch what the other players are doing, because you may have to play defense and block their rows.

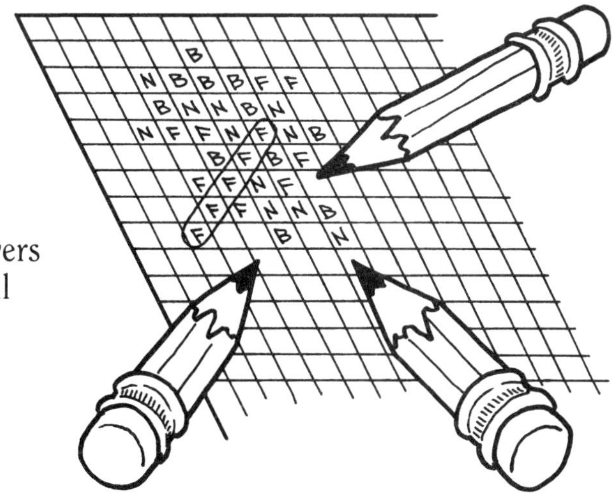

❹ Play until one of the players gets "five in a line," or until all the squares are filled. Then draw up another game board and play again!

30 FACE RACE

Find out who the best artist is in this hilarious portrait game! Whether or not your pictures even look human, it's lots of fun.

WHAT YOU'LL NEED

- two or more players
- pen or pencil
- paper
- hard surface
- colored pencils or pens (optional)

HOW TO PLAY

1. Each player has four minutes to draw a person that the other players know. It can be a famous person, such as a past president or a movie star, a cartoon or other fictional character, or someone in your town, such as a teacher or minister.

2. Be as detailed as possible. For example, if the person you are drawing has a distinguishing feature, such as a wart, a pointy beard, or a baseball cap that's seemingly attached to his or her head, be sure to add that to the picture. It'll make it easier for the other players to guess, and everyone will think you're a great artist!

3. Take turns guessing who the other players drew. Whoever identifies the most people in the pictures wins. And when you're done, give the pictures to the people you've drawn!

32 THE STORY OF YOUR LIFE

If you've ever thought about writing your life's story, here's how you can write the craziest autobiography of all time!

WHAT YOU'LL NEED

- scissors
- pen or pencil
- several sheets of paper
- flat, hard surface

Never use scissors in a moving vehicle, especially a car, bus, or train. Cut out what you need before you leave.

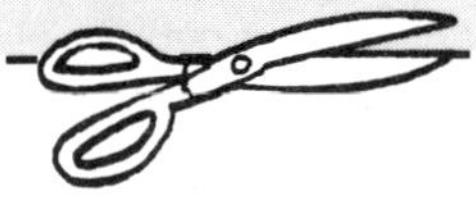

BEFORE YOU LEAVE

Cut up several long strips of paper, at least 30 to 40 strips. The strips should be at least an inch wide and long enough to write a whole sentence. Store these in your travel supply box until your trip.

HOW TO PLAY

1. Take your strips of paper and pen and start writing the story of your life. Use a strip of paper for each new sentence. Include where you were born, important and funny things that have happened to you, information about your family, and anything else that's meaningful to you.

2. Now here's the twist. Once you are finished with your life story, throw all the sentences into a hat or your travel supply box. Mix them up, and pick out one line at a time. Place them down on a flat surface in the order you picked them out.

3. Grab an audience and read your story. Be sure to read it in the order you picked the sentences. You can bet it's going to be goofy! You might even be born after you started school!

ONE STEP FURTHER

Try this game with any story or fairy tale you can think of, and see what crazy tales you will create!

33 MUTANT PAPER DOLL PUPPETS

Would your ears look better if they were attached to your elbows? How about a foot coming out of your forehead? Here's your chance to redesign the human body—make it as silly or as sensible as you want!

WHAT YOU'LL NEED

- lightweight cardboard (such as old telephone book covers)
- a magazine or two
- scissors
- glue
- tape
- popsicle sticks or pencils
- lap desk (optional)

Never use scissors in a moving vehicle, especially a car, bus, or train. Cut out what you need before you leave.

BEFORE YOU LEAVE

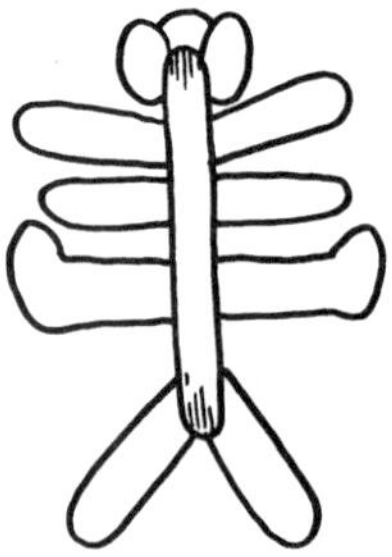

1. Cut out pages from magazines that have pictures of people or parts of the body. Choose faces, arms, legs, feet, and so on, in all different sizes. Cut out the individual body parts.

2. Glue all the pieces to the cardboard and cut those out. You should now have several separate body parts on pieces of cardboard. Store them in your travel box until your trip.

HOW TO PLAY

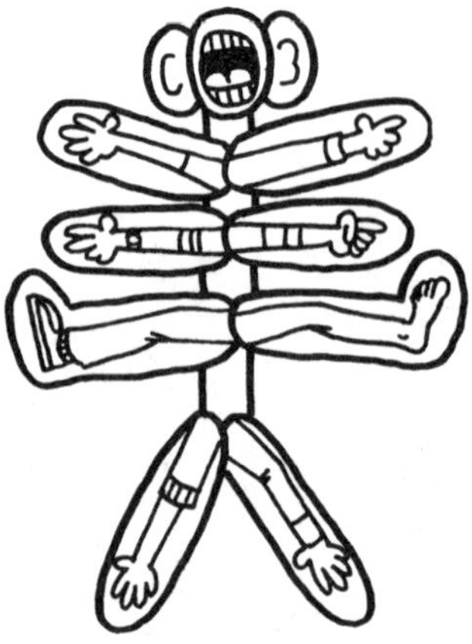

1. On your lap or lap desk, arrange selected cut-out body parts any wacky way you want. Give your creature eight arms, toes instead of fingers—anything goes!

2. Tape or glue the body parts together on a popsicle stick or pencil, as shown. Make a whole army of mutants!

3. Finally, put on goofy mutant alien plays for each other!

34 TRAVEL PASSWORD

This fun word game is sure to increase your vocabulary as you and a teammate compete for the grand password prize.

WHAT YOU'LL NEED

- four or more players
- 3-by-5-inch index cards
- hat
- pen or pencil
- sheet of paper

HOW TO PLAY

1 Divide into two teams, Team A and Team B. Each team then writes down on an index card what it wants if it wins the game. (The teams should keep their prize cards a secret.) A prize might be "Get a foot massage from the losers," "Watch the losers feed each other ice cream while blindfolded," or anything else you can think of. But be careful—these "password prizes" are put in a hat and mixed up, so if you lose, you may end up having to act out your own "prize"!

2 Now Team A and Team B each write down five words—two nouns, two verbs, and one adjective—on separate index cards. Then Team A players put their cards facedown in front of Team B, and vice versa.

3 To begin the game, one player on Team A takes a card from the deck in front of his or her team. This player gives one-word hints to his or her team partners, trying to get them to guess the word written on the card. Here's the catch: Only noun hints may be given for nouns, verb hints for verbs, and adjective hints for adjectives. And you can't use any form of the word in your hint! For example, let's say the word on the card is "run," a verb. The verb hints might be "sprint," "dash," "jog," "race," and "hustle."

4 For every hint a player gives, the teammates have to take one guess at the answer. Each wrong guess adds one point to the team's score. The maximum number of clues that can be received on a word is five.

❺ After a correct guess or five clues, write down the points. Here's how to determine the score:

If the word is guessed after the first clue, you receive no points.
If the word is guessed after the second clue, you receive one point.
If the word is guessed after the third clue, you receive two points.
If the word is guessed after the fourth clue, you receive three points.
If the word is guessed after the fifth clue, you receive four points.

❻ Now a member from Team B takes a card and tries to get the Team B players to guess the word. After each team goes through five words, add up the score. In this game, the team with the *least* number of points wins! Don't forget to let the winning team pick the password prize from the hat.

35 ON-THE-SPOT DOT-TO-DOT

1

You don't need to be an incredible artist to create great works of dot-to-dot art! Make your own dot-to-dot puzzles, then give it to a younger brother or sister who just can't seem to sit still. (Your parents will be forever in your debt!)

WHAT YOU'LL NEED

- favorite magazine with pictures
- pen or pencil
- tracing paper

HOW TO PLAY

❶ Find a picture in your magazine that you want to use for your dot-to-dot puzzle. Try using a picture of a famous person or building.

❷ Put the paper on top of the picture and trace over it. Don't use straight or crooked lines, just dots. Be careful not to make the dots too close together; otherwise, your sibling will guess the picture before he or she even does the activity. Leave about ½ inch to 1 inch between each dot.

❸ Once you have finished outlining the picture with dots, number the dots, starting with 1 and continuing on, assigning each dot a consecutive number.

❹ Now give it to a younger brother or sister to connect the dots. Can he or she guess the picture you traced? Who cares? It's great fun—and it keeps him or her out of your hair!

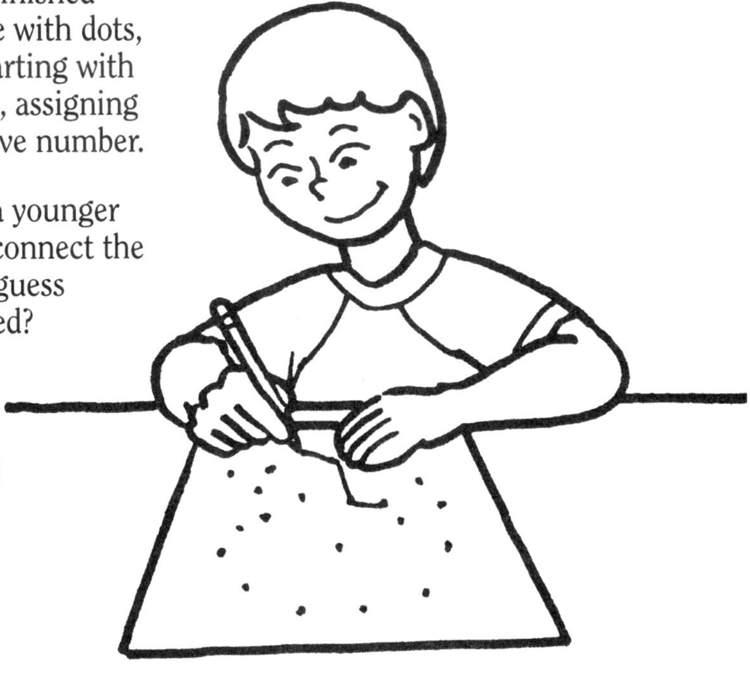

36 NAMES-OF-FAME CHAIN

Here's a game that will test your knowledge of famous people, whether they're real or make-believe! The biggest name-dropper wins!

WHAT YOU'LL NEED

- two or more players

HOW TO PLAY

1. One player starts by naming a famous person in history, the movies, rap music, books, or anything else you can think of.

2. The next player must name another famous person whose first name starts with the first letter of the last name of the previous famous person. Confused? Don't be—it's easy! If the first person says "George Washington," the next person has to say "William Shakespeare" or another name starting with "W."

3. Then the following person has to say "Sylvester Stallone" or another "S" name. Remember, they don't have to be real people, just famous names! Even "Roger Rabbit" will do! See how many names you can connect together, but if you can't think of one, you're out!

37 WHAT'S THE WORD?

Here's another word game that will have you under its "spell." Can you fill in the missing letters and guess the word before the other players do?

WHAT YOU'LL NEED

- two or more players
- dictionary
- paper
- pen or pencil

HOW TO PLAY

1. Choose one player to be the "Word Master." That player looks up a word and its definition in the dictionary. Long, uncommon words are best, but make sure the word is not *too* impossible!

2. The Word Master writes the word on a piece of paper, leaving out the first letter and every other letter after that. He or she also underlines the spaces where the missing letters belong.

3. Next, the Word Master writes a one- or two-word definition below the word. For example, if the player chooses the word "cantankerous," he or she would write "_ A _ T _ N _ E _ O _ S" and underneath it would write "bad-tempered."

4. With more than two players, the players take turns guessing letters to fill in the missing spaces. One correct letter guess fills in only one space, so you can guess the same letter more than once.

5. Each correct guess is worth one point and another turn. After a wrong guess, it's the next player's turn.

6. Continue taking turns guessing letters. The player who figures out the word first and correctly guesses it receives five points. Any player who guesses at the word and gets it wrong loses two points and his or her turn.

❼ After five rounds with five different words, add up the scores. The one with the most points wins and becomes the next Word Master. Now play again!

ONE STEP FURTHER

Once everyone becomes a Word Master extraordinaire, try the game with whole phrases instead of words. Like this: “ _ N / _ P _ L _ / A / _ A _ / K _ E _ S / _ H _ / D _ C _ O _ / A _ A _.” The hint: “medical advice.” Can you guess what it is?

38 DO YOU REMEMBER?

Do you have a photographic memory? Find out with this game that gives your travel-weary brain cells a real workout!

WHAT YOU'LL NEED

- two or more players
- shoe box or paper bag
- several sheets of paper
- 15 small items per player
- pens or pencils (one per player)
- watch or clock with a second hand
- travel supply box

HOW TO PLAY

1. First, everyone collects 15 different small items and stores them in a shoe box or paper bag. You can do this either before you leave or on the road. Make sure to keep your items secret from everyone else! Some possible items: small shiny rocks, coins, leaves, spools of thread, flowers, napkins, and erasers. (Unusual items are especially good to collect, but please, no bugs!)

2. Hand out paper and pencils or pens to everyone. Pick one player to spread all of his or her items on the lid of the travel supply box so that everyone can see them. After 30 seconds, the player then puts the items back into the bag or box.

3. Now each player has two minutes to write down as many of the items as he or she can remember. No fair peeking at anyone else's list!

4. After the time is up, the person with the objects takes the items out of the bag or box one at a time. The players should give themselves a point for each correct object that is written down. The player with the most correctly listed items wins!

5. Now let the next player put his or her items in the lid, and start the game again!

39 AUTO-BIOGRAPHY

Use long hours spent traveling in a car to create a story that you not only write, but illustrate, too!

WHAT YOU'LL NEED

- several sheets of paper
- old magazine
- pen or pencil
- glue
- stapler or tape
- photo of yourself (optional)

HOW TO PLAY

1. Go through an old magazine, looking for pictures to illustrate the things that have happened in your life. Choose pictures of babies, houses, schools, and so on.

2. Tear out each picture carefully, and use them in place of words you would write. You can write a few words, then paste in a picture. For instance, the first line of your story may be, "When I was a little girl, I couldn't even tie my own shoes." Then, you'd find a picture of a girl and some shoes and *replace* the pictures with the words.

3. Keep on writing and finding pictures, tearing them out, and pasting them on consecutive pieces of paper, until you've finished your story. Soon you will have a fully illustrated story about you!

4. Finally, make your story into a real book by binding the left side of the pages with staples or tape (make sure your pages are in the correct order). Name your story and illustrate a cover. Don't forget to paste in a photo of yourself!

40 MYSTERY MESSAGES

2

Have you ever wanted to get a message to your brothers, sisters, or friends that only they could read? Here's a way! Only someone with the code breaker (that you create!) will be able to figure out your "top secret information."

WHAT YOU'LL NEED

- two or more players
- old magazines
- sheet of paper
- pen or pencil
- glue or tape

HOW TO PLAY

1. Think of a message to send, such as: "Meet me at the motel pool at 5 P.M.," "Let's ditch Michelle at the truck stop," or "Brian has termites."

2. Find the words you need in a magazine and carefully tear them out.

3. Scramble the words and arrange them on a piece of paper. Now, your message might read something like this: "motel P.M. at meet pool me the 5 at."

4. Glue or tape the words on the paper and write a number to the right of each word. For example, the message would now read: "motel (1) P.M. (2) at (3) meet (4) pool (5) me (6) the (7) 5 (8) at (9)". Feel safe passing the message around, because no one will know what it means—yet!

5. Next, write the code breaker that only you and your chosen pal will have access to. To do this, write down the numbers that are next to the words in the order that the words *should* read. For example, the code breaker for the message illustrated here would read: "4 6 3 7 1 5 9 8 2."

6. Then, give the code breaker to your co-conspirator. Once he or she has both the coded message and the code breaker, your co-conspirator can put the two together to figure out the message.

41 BRAT CAGE

When, after hours on the road, your bratty little brother and sister are driving you crazy, use this "cage" to tame their pesky personalities!

WHAT YOU'LL NEED

- photo of your brother or sister (or any other brat!)
- scissors
- cardboard
- yarn, about 4 feet
- glue
- pencil or markers

Never use scissors in a moving vehicle, especially a car, bus, or train. Cut out what you need before you leave.

BEFORE YOU LEAVE

Cut the cardboard into a circle big enough to fit the photo on. Poke two holes, one on each end of the cardboard. Cut the yarn into two pieces, each about 2 feet long.

HOW TO PLAY

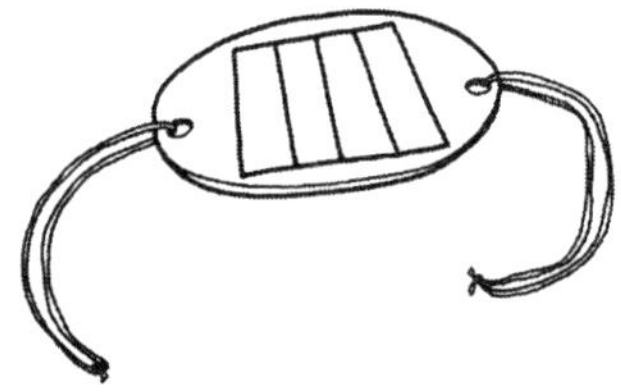

1. On one side of the cardboard, draw a box and five thick black lines going across from top to bottom. These are the "bars" to the prison.

2. Glue the photo to the other side of the cardboard.

3. Thread one piece of yarn into one of the holes on the cardboard, then tie the yarn in a loop. Do the same with the other side. This should give you a loop of yarn on both ends of the circle.

4. Next, hold the ends of the yarn in your hands. Twirl the cardboard circle around and around to wind it up, then pull the two pieces of yarn outward so the cardboard circle spins around. As the circle flips around, the alternating photo and "bars" will make it look as if you have the pesky person locked up in a cage!

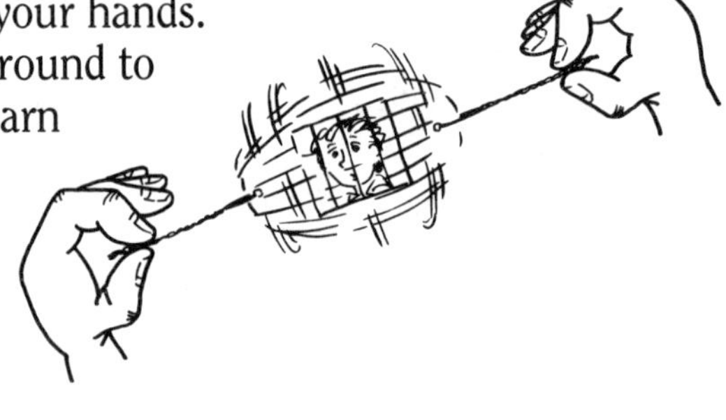

42 PUT YOUR TRIP ON THE MAP QUIZ

Here's a terrific way to draw cool maps, play a game, and remember your journey—all at the same time.

WHAT YOU'LL NEED

- two players
- paper
- pen or pencil

HOW TO PLAY

1. To start, both players need a piece of paper and a pen or pencil. You draw the map first and the other player is the quiz contestant.

2. Begin by drawing a map of what you see as you travel. Don't leave out anything—big cross streets, highways, bridges, rivers, lakes, mountains, and buildings. Draw quickly, but accurately. Make any notes you think might be important, such as city names, landmarks, or even interesting scenery you pass.

3. At the same time, the other player takes notes on what he or she sees along the way, concentrating on as many landmarks and as much scenery as possible.

4. After approximately 20 minutes, or after drawing 30 to 40 sites, stop drawing. Then make a neat copy of the map you've just drawn. Only this time, write in the names of only half the landmarks and other map entries, and draw in blank lines next to other half (at least 20) of the sites. These blanks will be filled in by the quiz taker.

5. Now hand the map with the blanks to the other player. Using only his or her notes, the quiz taker must fill in the names of the landmarks in the blanks. Here's how to score your quiz:

    16 to 20 correct: Excellent! Consider a career in navigation!
    11 to 15 correct: Very good! You could lead the expedition.
    6 to 10 correct: Not so hot. Back to map school!
    0 to 5 correct: Watch out—you might get lost in your own backyard!

6. Now switch positions and play again!

43 WHAT AN ANIMAL! 1

Have your parents or teachers ever told you to "stop acting like an animal?" It's usually a good idea, *except* when you're playing this game!

WHAT YOU'LL NEED

- four or more players
- scratch paper
- pen or pencil
- 2 hats or small boxes

HOW TO PLAY

1. Divide into two teams. Each team writes down the names of 10 animals on 10 small scraps of paper. Pick animals that are a little out of the ordinary, such as an orangutan or a crocodile.

2. When the teams are finished, each should place the scraps of paper into two different hats or boxes. It is important to keep the teams' animals separate from each other.

3. To begin, one player from one team chooses a piece of paper from the other team's hat or box. Without saying anything, he or she must act like the animal written on the paper and try to get his or her teammates to guess that animal.

4. If the teammates are having a difficult time figuring out the animal, the player can also make animal sounds. Each team receives three points for guessing the animal if no sounds are made, and one point if sounds are used. Whichever team earns the most points wins.

44 LICENSE PLATE LOTTO

You may not win millions of dollars with this version of lotto, but you'll win your friends' admiration when you're the lotto champion!

WHAT YOU'LL NEED

- three or more players
- pen or pencil
- ruler
- scratch paper
- several pieces of light-colored construction paper (at least one per player)

PREPARING THE GAME BOARD

1. First, you need to make a game board for each player. To make a board, take a sheet of construction paper. Use a ruler to draw six lines across and six lines vertical, with about an inch space between each line. This should give you 25 squares.

2. Now each player fills in each box with a letter. Any letter of the alphabet can be used, but a letter can't be used more than twice on one board.

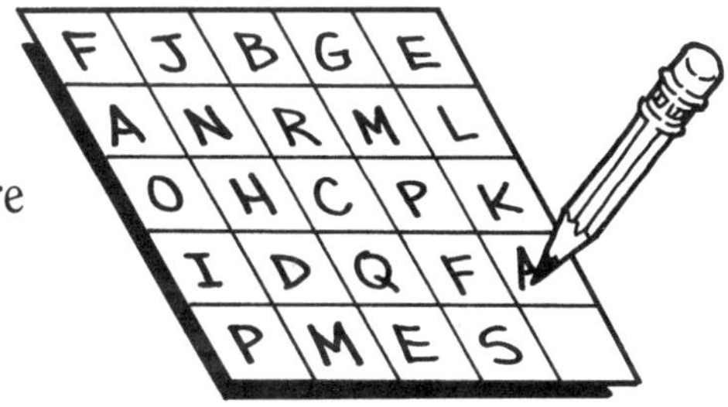

HOW TO PLAY

1. Choose one person to be the caller. Mix up all the game boards, and give one to each player except the caller. The players should also have a piece of scratch paper that they can tear into small pieces.

2. When the caller sees a passing car, he or she will announce the first letter on the license plate. So, if the license plate reads "2XRT436," the letter called would be "X."

3. Any player with that letter on his or her board, tears off a small piece of scratch paper and covers the spot. Only one letter can be covered per call, so if the letter called is "A" and you have two "A's" on your board, you can cover only one of them.

4. The first player to cover all the letters and fill the game board wins! Be sure the winner shouts "LPL!" (License Plate Lotto).

5. The winner now becomes the caller, and you can start the game all over again.

45 LOONY TUNE-Y

While this game may not lead you into a career in music, it will definitely lead you to laughter!

WHAT YOU'LL NEED

- two or more players
- pen or pencil
- paper

HOW TO PLAY

1. To start, all the players agree on a familiar tune, such as "Happy Birthday."

2. Once that's decided, everyone writes down his or her own funny new words to the song. All the verses should be about family members, teachers, friends, or someone else that everybody in the group knows—even your dog!

3. Go around in a circle and let each player take a turn singing his or her own unique version. Each player should sing only a verse or two so that the game moves along quickly.

4. Want an example? Pretend the lyrics are about a friend named Joe, and the melody is from the song "Row, Row, Row Your Boat." The song could go something like this:

Joe, Joe, Joe is twelve;
He thinks he's really cool;
Terribly, terribly, terribly, terribly;
He's rather quite a fool!

Silly enough for you? Start singing!

46 STUMP A STRANGER

1

PARENTAL SUPERVISION REQUIRED

Here are three wacky word gags! Have a contest with your brother or sister to see who can stump the most people.

WHAT YOU'LL NEED

- two or more players
- paper
- pen

HOW TO PLAY

1. The gags listed below have been around a long time. You get five points for each gag you pull off successfully. If the person guesses the joke correctly, you receive one point for getting the person to play along. You must take turns with your opponents.

2. The only rule in this game is that you can ask only one person one of the gags. Otherwise, that person is likely to catch on to the gags. You can ask a server at a restaurant, a gas station attendant, cousins you visit, anyone! *However, never approach a stranger by yourself.* A parent should be with you at all times.

3. When you find someone to play the game with, always ask the person first if he or she has a minute for a good gag. If the person doesn't have time, don't bother him or her.

GAG 1

You begin by saying "Say stop." The other person says "Stop." You say "Say go." The other person says "Go." Repeat this about five times or so, keeping a rapid pace. Then, when the other person expects you to say "Say stop," you say "What do you do at a green light?" Usually, the person will say "Stop" and you got 'em!

GAG 2

You say "Say toast," and the person says "Toast." You say "Say most," and the person says "Most." Once again, you'll want to repeat these about five times or so at a quick pace. Then, instead of saying "Say toast" again, you say "What do you put in the toaster?" The person will probably say "Toast!" And you say "Nope, you put bread in a toaster!"

GAG 3

You say "Say black." The person says "Black." You say "Say white." The person says "White." Repeat this a few times, and then say "What do cows drink?" You can bet the person will say, "Milk!" And you say "Nope, cows don't drink milk, they give it!"

ONE STEP FURTHER

After you've done the gags listed for a while, make up some of your own!

47 BOMBS AWAY

Destroy your enemy's buildings before your enemy destroys yours in this wild war game! You don't have to be a military genius to play, but victory will go to the player with the most accurate bombers.

WHAT YOU'LL NEED

- two players
- pen or pencil
- 8½-by-11-inch graph paper or 8½-by-11-inch plain paper and ruler

PREPARING FOR THE GAME

❶ Each player needs his or her own blueprint to "build" a city. If graph paper isn't available, draw 11 lines down and 11 lines across on your paper to make 100 squares. The lines should be about ½ inch apart.

❷ Number the columns of squares going down (1 through 10) and assign letters (A through J) to the rows going across. Write "Home Base" across the top of the paper.

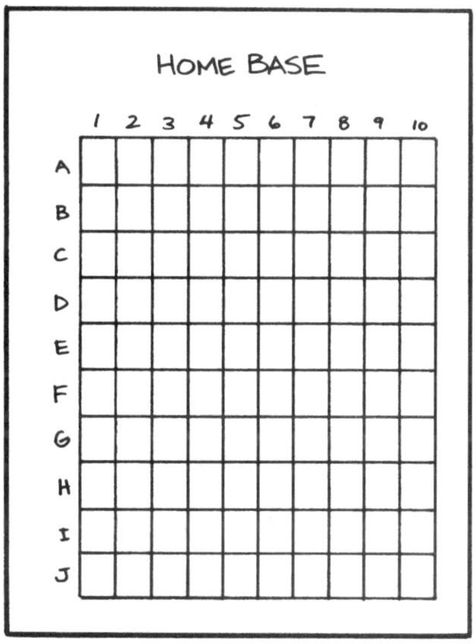

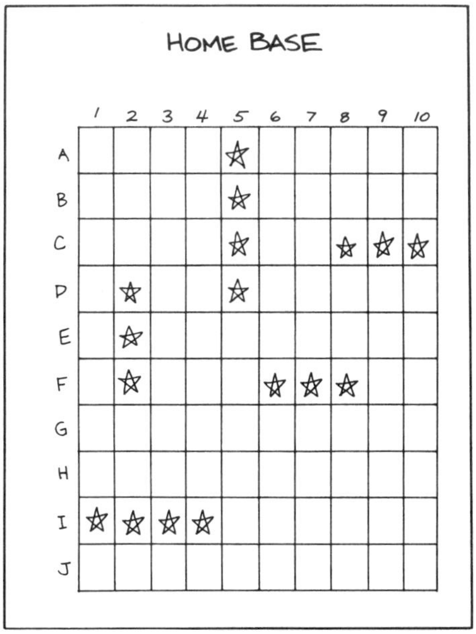

❸ Each player gets five buildings to draw in. Draw in three buildings that take up three squares each and two that use four squares each. Place them anywhere you like in your city. They can go up and down or sideways (not diagonally). Mark the placement of your buildings with stars, as the picture here shows. Important: Don't let your opponent see your map!

HOW TO PLAY

❶ The object of the game is to bomb all of your opponent's buildings that are marked on his or her map. To begin, Player One calls out a letter/number combination, such as "4-A." If Player Two has a star drawn in that square, he says, "On target," and places an "X" in that square on his board. At the same time, Player One draws an "X" in that square on her board to represent a hit. But, if Player One calls out a letter/number combination, and none of Player Two's buildings are in that square, it's a miss, and Player Two says, "Off target." Player Two doesn't mark anything on his board, but Player One marks her miss with a big "O" on her board in the appropriate spot.

❷ Players continue taking turns, answering "On target" for a hit and "Off target" for a miss, and keeping track on the charts. If Player One wipes out all the sections in one of Player Two's buildings, Player Two says, "Out of action." (See the example in the illustration in row I, columns 1 through 4.)

❸ The player to wipe out all of his or her opponent's buildings first is the winner! Bombs away!

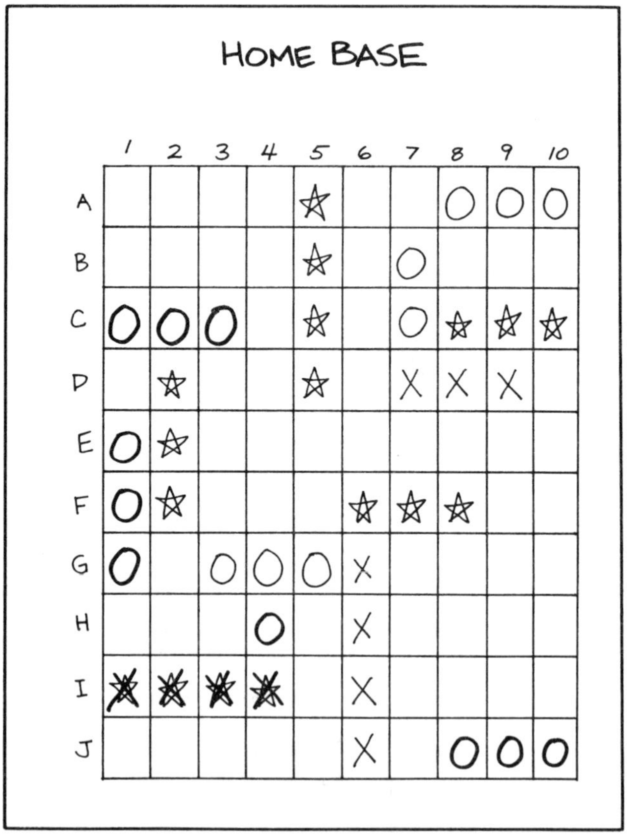

48 THUMPER

Ready to make some noise as you sharpen your memory and your coordination? This game will have you clapping, singing, gesturing, and thumping until you find yourselves abandoned at a rest stop just outside Okoboji!

WHAT YOU'LL NEED

- three or more players

HOW TO PLAY

1. Each player chooses a gesture that will be his or her gesture. For example, with three players:

   #1 may choose grabbing his or her ears
   #2 may choose clapping his or her hands
   #3 may choose covering his or her eyes

2. Then all players agree on one "transition" gesture, like holding their noses. Choose one player to be "It." This person will start the game.

3. Now, everyone starts drumming on their thighs—THUMPING—and . . .

   "It": "What's the name of the game?"
   Other players: "THUMPER!"
   "It": "How do you play it?"
   Other players: "Thump it!"

4. Then "It" does his or her gesture, followed by the "transition" gesture, followed by another player's gesture. The player whose gesture came last goes next, and on it goes. Here's an example:

   "It" grabs his ears, then holds his nose, and finally, claps his hands. Clapping hands is #2's gesture, so #2 then claps her hands, holds her nose, then covers her eyes. Covering eyes is #3's gesture, so #3 covers his eyes, then holds his nose, and either grabs his ears or claps his hands.

All the while, the players keep thumping their thighs with their hands. Whoever misses a gesture, gets a gesture in the wrong order, or forgets one is out. You can go in any order, and you can even pick yourself! See how fast you can go, and have a THUMPING good time!

49 ARMCHAIR FOOTBALL

If you like the fast action of football, you'll love this version of football played with dice! Go for the bomb, run back a kickoff, block a punt, and score, score, score! You can play by yourself or with another fan!

WHAT YOU'LL NEED

- small piece of cardboard
- scissors
- paper
- pair of dice
- ruler
- pen or pencil
- a little football knowledge

Never use scissors in a moving vehicle, especially a car, bus, or train. Cut out what you need before you leave.

BEFORE YOU LEAVE

Cut out a ball marker and a first-down marker from cardboard. The ball marker should be a triangle, and the first-down marker should be a rectangle exactly 1 inch wide.

PREPARING FOR THE GAME

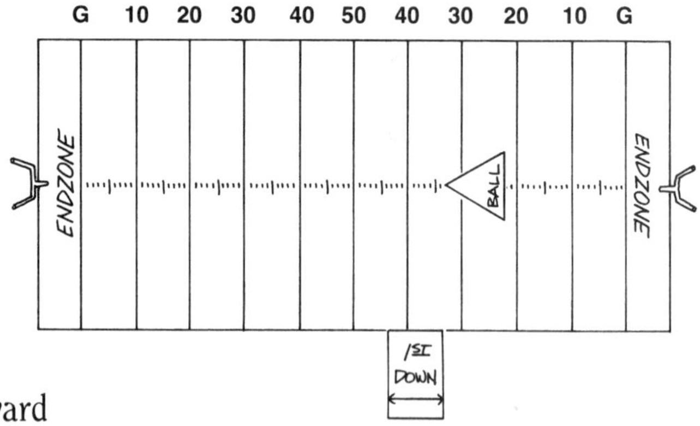

1 First, you need to prepare your field. With a ruler, draw a large rectangle on a piece of paper and mark off the end zones and all the 10-yard lines. Each 10-yard line should be 1 inch apart. Also draw in the "hash marks." Those are the short lines that mark every yard on the field.

2 Now draw a scoreboard on a separate sheet of paper. It should look like this:

TEAM	1	2	3	4	FINAL

HOW TO PLAY

1 Here are three rules to remember and to read at the start of the game: 1) If a play goes past the end zone (such as a 60-yard pass from the 20-yard line), it's a touchdown; 2) if a punt goes into the end zone, it's a touchback and comes out to the return team's 20-yard line; and 3) if a field goal is no good, the defensive team immediately receives the ball where it lays (this is called the line of scrimmage).

2 Refer to the following charts for all the plays. The number on the left stands for the sum of the two dice rolled for each play. You may want to copy these charts onto separate pieces of paper for easy reference.

RUN

2 = TOUCHDOWN!
3 = Big hole! 10-yard gain
4 = 3-yard loss
5 = 4-yard gain
6 = Big pile up! 2-yard gain
7 = 6-yard loss
8 = 5-yard gain
9 = Stopped cold! No gain
10 = Good move! 17-yard gain
11 = No blocking! 5-yard loss
12 = 25-yard gain

PUNT

2-4 = 20 yards
5-6 = 60 yards
7-8 = 45 yards
9-12 = 30 yards

FIELD GOAL

2-7 = Blocked! Other team gains control
8-12 = Good! (Player must be at least at his or her own 40-yard line to attempt a field goal)

PASS

2 = Bomb! 60-yard gain
3 = Intercepted—it's the other team's ball at the 50
4 = On target! 15-yard gain
5 = Incomplete pass
6 = 10-yard gain
7 = Stopped cold! No gain
8 = Incomplete pass
9 = Sack! 8-yard loss
10 = Incomplete pass
11 = Post pattern! 20-yard gain
12 = Bomb! 40-yard gain

KICKOFF RETURN

2 = Down the sideline! TOUCHDOWN
3-4 = Returned to return team's 40-yard line
5-9 = Returned to return team's 20-yard line
10-12 = Returned to return team's 30-yard line

❸ Now you're ready to play. Flip a coin to see who kicks off and who receives. Then each player takes one dice, and the game is on. If you're playing alone, you'll roll both dice (for the offense and defense). To kick off, both players roll their dice and use the "Kickoff Return" chart to see where to place the ball. Point the ball marker to the spot and place the edge of the first-down marker along the sideline, beginning at that spot as well. This will show the offensive team how far he or she needs to go to get a first down.

❹ Next, the offensive player announces if the next play is going to be a run or a pass. Both players roll their dice and check either the "Run" chart or the "Pass" chart. For instance, the offensive player calls a run and the roll of both dice equals a five. This gives the offensive team a four-yard gain, so the player should move the ball marker up four yards to mark the spot. Now it's second down and six yards to go for the first down. If the next play is a pass and the roll is a ten, the offense has an incomplete pass. Now it's third down, and there are still six yards to go for a first down.

❺ Each quarter lasts for 20 plays, so keep a count of the plays on the sheet of paper that has the scoreboard. Kickoffs and punts also count as plays. Drive up the field, punt, kick a field goal, or score a touchdown! At the end of each quarter, write in the score on your scoreboard. Play hard, play clean, and may the best team win!

50 BUSINESS CARD BONANZA!

You and your pals will mean business when it comes to seeing who can win this collector's game!

WHAT YOU'LL NEED

- small box or paper sack

HOW TO PLAY

1. The object of this game is to see who can collect the most business cards and free memorabilia during your trip. Make sure that all participants understand the rules below, then start collecting!

2. Every place you go, tuck a business card, restaurant napkin, or a hotel and entertainment brochure into your box or sack. Each of these items count as one point. You cannot count any item that you paid for, and you cannot take anything that is not supposed to be given away, such as ashtrays or hotel towels.

3. As you collect the souvenirs, try to be secretive. If all the participants see what everyone else is taking, then everyone will end up with the same items. Keep all your items hidden away.

4. Once you get home, or reach a certain destination in your journey, everyone should count up all the business cards, napkins, brochures, and other free memorabilia he or she has collected. Whoever has the most wins! (But in "Business Card Bonanza," everyone really wins, because everyone ends up with loads of free souvenirs from every place visited!)

51 ON YOUR MARK... GET SET...

1

Another vacation. Another long, boring ride in a car, plane, train, boat, or however you travel. But it doesn't have to be that way. This book is full of fun and creative ways to pass the time until you get to your destination. But before you start traveling, there are a few things you'll need to do to prepare for your trip.

WHAT YOU'LL NEED

- plain canvas tote bag or laundry bag
- fabric markers or paints
- pencil
- game supplies for trip
- poster board (optional)
- grease pencil (optional)
- flat board or lap desk (optional)

BEFORE YOU LEAVE

1. There are many activities that don't require supplies—word and memory games, sing-alongs, strategy matches, and more. Others will require a few simple supplies, such as pencils, pens, rulers, crayons, scissors, glue, and tape. Only a few activities will need special game pieces. Look through this book and collect what you need to play the games that appeal to you.

2. Next grab the canvas tote bag or laundry bag to make a one-of-a-kind travel tote bag for storing your supplies. With a pencil, write on the bag: (your first name)'S TRAVEL BAG. Place a piece of cardboard inside to protect the back side of the bag. Then paint over the penciled lines with fabric markers or paint. If you like, add some other designs—maybe a tic-tac-toe game grid, or outlines of cars, trucks, trains, and planes. When the bag is dry, it's ready to fill.

Note: If you need to cut something for any of the projects in this book, never use scissors or other sharp objects when the car is moving. It is too dangerous. So whenever you see the box below, it means do any cutting before you leave on your trip.

Never use scissors in a moving vehicle, especially a car, bus, or train. Cut out what you need before you leave.

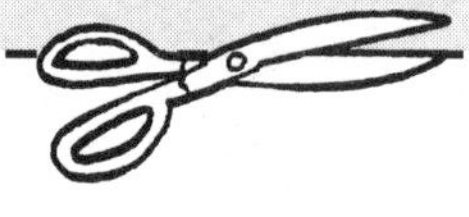

NOW...LET'S GO!

52

BOX IT UP

Keep making these boxes and you won't have to worry about being sent to the "losers" box!

WHAT YOU'LL NEED

- two or more players
- pen or pencil for each player
- $8\frac{1}{2}$-by-11-inch graph paper or $8\frac{1}{2}$-by-11-inch plain paper and ruler

HOW TO PLAY

1. First you need to draw your game board. Select one player to draw ten rows of ten dots across the piece of graph paper to make 100 dots. If graph paper isn't available, use a ruler to mark off dots on a plain piece of paper. The dots should be about $\frac{1}{2}$ inch apart.

2. The first player draws a line between any two dots, either vertical or horizontal. Then the next player draws a line, either connected to the line just drawn or somewhere else on the page.

3. Players continue taking turns drawing lines. The goal is for each player to complete as many four-sided boxes as possible. Once a player completes a box, he or she writes his or her initials inside the box, then takes an extra turn.

4. When no more lines can be drawn, count up the boxes each player has captured. The player with the most boxes wins!

ONE STEP FURTHER

For a change of pace, play Don't Box It Up. In this game, the object is *not* to complete a box. If three sides are already completed, you *must* complete the square. If you don't, your opponent can complete it for you and add your initials to the box. The player with the most boxes is the loser in this version.

53 BLOCK BY BLOCK

It took hundreds of years to build the ancient pyramids of Egypt block by block. How long will it take you to build a pyramid of words?

WHAT YOU'LL NEED

- two or more players
- paper
- pen or pencil
- ruler

HOW TO PLAY

1. To begin, each player draws a pyramid of blocks on a sheet of paper. The top row of the pyramid has two blocks, the second row three blocks, and so on. The last layer is seven blocks wide.

2. Now choose a category, such as "TV Shows" or "Travel Words."

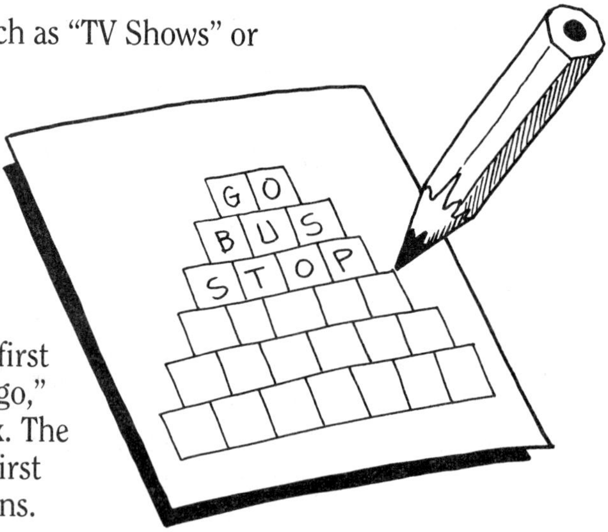

3. When everyone is ready, one player yells "Go." Each player starts filling each pyramid row with words whose letters fit the number of boxes. For example, say the chosen category is "Travel Words." The first word in the pyramid might be "go," with each letter occupying a box. The next word might be "bus." The first player to complete a pyramid wins.

ONE STEP FURTHER

Add more words by changing your pyramid to a diamond. To do this, first make a pyramid. After the last row of seven blocks, start going down with a six-box row, a five-box row, and so on, until you reach the final two-box row.

54 MILK MONEY

Try this fun travel version of the popular game Pogs™.

WHAT YOU'LL NEED

- two or more players
- cardboard
- scissors
- cap from a one-gallon plastic milk jug
- markers or crayons
- shoe box

BEFORE YOU LEAVE

1. Take the cap from a one-gallon plastic milk jug (or something else of a similar size) and trace the shape onto the cardboard, making five coins for each player. Then cut out the coins with your scissors.

2. Use your markers or crayons to draw animals, faces, or weird designs on the coins. Make sure to draw only on *one side* of the coins. Leave the other side blank.

HOW TO PLAY

1. First flip one of the handmade coins to see who goes first. Then each player puts five coins face down in the shoe box. Replace the lid. Heads is the side with the design. Tails is the blank side of the coin.

2. The first player shakes the box for three seconds, then removes the lid. All the coins that land heads *up* belong to that player. The next player takes his or her turn shaking the box and winning coins. Continue taking turns until all the coins have been won.

3. If the number of coins that turns up equals the number of players, that player loses all of his or her coins. For example, if three players are in the game and a player turns up three coins, that player must put all of the coins he or she has won back into the box.

4. The player with the most coins at the end of the game wins.

55 ANY WHICH WAY YOU ADD IT

Any which way you play this number brainteaser, it's sure to add up to hours of fun!

WHAT YOU'LL NEED

- paper, 8½ by 11 inches
- pencil
- flat board or lap desk

HOW TO PLAY

❶ To begin, each player folds a piece of paper into nine sections, like a tic-tac-toe grid. Tear the paper on the fold lines to make nine pieces of paper.

❷ Now players fill in each of the nine pieces of paper with one of the following numbers: 2, 4, 6, 8, 10, 12, 14, 16, and 18. Numbers can only be used once.

❸ On a flat surface, each player arranges the numbers so that any three numbers—in any direction (horizontal, vertical, or diagonal)—add up to thirty. The first player to solve the puzzle wins.

HINT: The secret to cracking this puzzle is finding the number that must be in the center box.

56 BACKSEAT THEATER

You won't miss television when you can act out your favorite stories in the backseat of the car. Shhh, the curtain is about to go up.

WHAT YOU'LL NEED

- old socks
- colorful buttons
- glue
- yarn
- lunch-size paper bags
- markers or crayons
- magazines
- scissors
- fabric scraps
- watch

Never use scissors in a moving vehicle, especially a car, bus, or train. Cut out what you need before you leave.

BEFORE YOU LEAVE

Each player makes one puppet. It can be anything you want—a princess, a prince, a monster, or frog! Make either a sock puppet or a paper bag puppet.

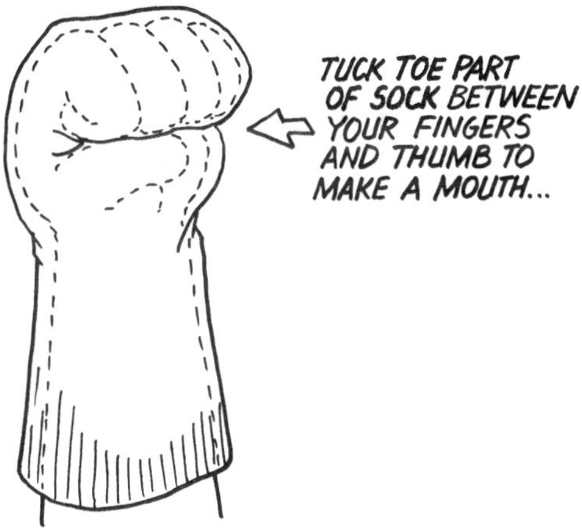

To make a sock puppet (ideal for creatures like dragons and snakes): Take an old sock and slide it over your hand. Tuck the toe part of the sock between your fingers and your thumb to make a mouth. With your free hand, mark places for the eyes and nose. Now slide the sock off your hand. On the top side of the sock, glue buttons on for eyes and a nose. Cut fabric scraps for scales or a tongue. Add a bit of yarn for a tuft of fur. If you want a well-dressed creature, tie a ribbon around its neck or add a bow tie. By moving your fingers and thumb, your sock puppet's "mouth" will move.

To make a paper bag puppet (ideal for human characters): Slide the sack over your hand. The folded bottom flap will be your puppet's face. Use your markers and crayons to draw eyes and a nose. Or, slide your hand out of the sack and cut out eyes, a nose, lips, and designs from old magazines and glue them onto the paper bag. To use, place your hand inside the paper bag and curve your four fingers into the flap. Move your fingers to move the puppet's mouth.

HOW TO PLAY

❶ Each player selects a story for his or her puppet to tell. It can be a retelling of a classic fairy tale, such as *Cinderella* or *Peter Pan,* or a reenactment of a scene from a favorite television show or movie. Or, a player can make up a completely original tale.

❷ Each player has three minutes to put on a short skit using his or her puppet. Be as dramatic as possible.

❸ After everyone has had a chance to perform, pick elements from each of the skits and combine them into a new skit using all of the puppets. This spur-of-the-moment performing is called improvisation.

❹ There are no winners or losers in the game. But this game is so much fun, everyone comes out a winner in the end!

57 SOUVENIR CAP

There's more than one way to save those memories of your trip. Put them on your head!

WHAT YOU'LL NEED

- old baseball cap
- glue
- souvenirs you gather from your trip

HOW TO PLAY

1. First find an old cap you'd like to decorate. Maybe it's a hat from a team you or one of your brothers or sisters played on.

2. If you plan on buying mementos to put on your cap, make a budget before the trip so you don't overspend on this project. You can find small items like state pins and stickers at many service stations.

3. Why not create a one-of-kind, didn't-cost-me-a-cent cap. They're the best kind, anyway. You can use *found* objects, like buttons, printed napkins, or wrappers from all the snacks you ate along the way. Use your imagination.

4. Now glue your mementos to your cap. With your memories so close to your head, you'll never forget them.

58 PHOTO FINISH

PARENTAL SUPERVISION REQUIRED

Grab your camera and concentrate on photographing your favorite things. You just might find out that you're a sure shot when it comes to taking a perfect snapshot!

WHAT YOU'LL NEED

- camera
- film
- notebook
- pen or pencil

HOW TO PLAY

❶ Decide what you want to photograph. Professional photographers often concentrate on one subject, such as flowers or trees. Here are a few suggestions:

old barns
service station signs
people wearing slogan T-shirts
farm animals
country roads
street signs

❷ Once you start shooting your subject, you may be tempted to wander off by yourself. Don't! *Always stay with a parent*. Poking into old places and unknown sites can be dangerous.

❸ Unless you have an instant camera, you'll have to wait to have your photos developed and printed. Keep a notebook with information about when and where your pictures were taken. You'll want to have all the facts handy when you exhibit your photo masterpieces to family and friends back home.

ONE STEP FURTHER

With your mom and dad's permission, use a video recorder to make your own movie. You can document your vacation across the country, or your trip to Grandma's.

59 BLIND PIG

When you're driving through farm country, take a really good look at those cute little pigs. Do you think you can draw a picture of one . . . blindfolded?

WHAT YOU'LL NEED

- two or more players
- paper, $8\frac{1}{2}$ by 11 inches
- pen or pencil for each player
- flat board or lap desk (optional)
- scarf or bandanna for each player

HOW TO PLAY

1. Each player grabs a piece of paper and a pen or pencil.

2. Next each player ties a blindfold (the scarf or bandanna) around his or her head. No peeking! Once everyone is blindfolded, each player draws the outline of a pig on his or her paper in *one continuous movement*. You *must not* lift your pencil off the paper. The only exception is at the end of the drawing when you place the pig's eye where you think it belongs.

3. After the drawings are finished, everyone takes off the blindfolds. Each player then tears his or her drawing into twenty pieces.

4. Each player passes his or her pieces to another player who tries to reassemble them as quickly as possible. The first player to complete the pig puzzle wins. Now, did anybody remember to bring a roll of tape?

60 MIKE'S SMELLY SOCKS

1

Need a good laugh? This hilarious game is guaranteed to make you chuckle. The only problem is, if you laugh, you lose!

WHAT YOU'LL NEED

- two or more players
- pencil
- paper
- lunch-size paper bag

HOW TO PLAY

1. Choose a player to be "It."

2. The other players make up a silly phrase for this player to say, such as "Mike's smelly socks" or "the dog's hairy paw." The funnier the phrase, the better.

3. Now the other players take turns asking "It" questions. "It" must only answer with the silly phrase and try not to laugh!

4. Impossible? Try it. Here's how a sample game might go:

"What do you brush your teeth with?" ("Mike's smelly socks.") "What's your favorite food?" ("Mike's smelly socks.") "What grows in your garden?" ("Mike's smelly socks.") "It" gets one point for each question answered without laughing.

5. After all the players have had a chance to be "It," count up the points and write down everyone's score. Keep playing until one player has 20 points. He or she is the winner.

61

POCKET CHANGE

Amaze family, friends, and strangers with your magical ability to not only guess their age, but also how much loose change is in their pockets!

WHAT YOU'LL NEED

- paper
- pencil
- calculator (optional)

HOW TO PLAY

1. First, on a separate piece of paper copy down the formula at the end of this game for easy reference. Give a friend a piece of paper and pencil. He or she will do most of the work.

2. Tell your friend that you're going to use a series of complicated calculations to come up with his or her age and how much pocket change he or she has. Make him or her think the trick is really hard, even though it's actually very simple.

3. Ask your friend to write down his or her age, then to double it and write down that number.

4. Now have your friend add 5 to the total and write down that number.

5. Next ask him or her to multiply the sum by 50.

6. Now have your friend subtract 365 from his or her total.

7. Finally ask him or her to add the amount of pocket change to that number. The amount has to be less than one dollar for the trick to work.

8. When your friend finishes, ask him or her to read the last number to you. Write it down on your own piece of paper and add 115. The first two digits of your answer represent your friend's age, the last two the amount of change in his or her pocket. For example, if your friend was twelve years old and had 99 cents, this is how the formula would work:

Your directions	*Calculations*
Age:	12
Now multiply by 2:	24
Add 5:	29
Multiply by 50:	1450
Subtract 365:	1085
Add change in pocket (99 cents):	1184
You add 115:	1299

It works every time (as long as your friend's math is right). Try it on someone else, like your mom or dad. But warn them, no lying about their age!

62 WHEEL OF FORTUNE TELLING

Wouldn't it be great to be able to predict the future? Or at least who will win the next game? Well, here's a game that only a fortune teller can predict.

WHAT YOU'LL NEED

- two or more players
- heavy paper, 8½ by 11 inches
- crayons or markers, one different color per player
- scarf or bandanna

HOW TO PLAY

1 First have one player draw a large spoked wheel with sixteen equal pie-shaped wedges on a piece of paper. Then write fortunes in each wedge. You can use the suggestions here or make up your own:

"Win 1 point."

"Lose 1 point."

"Receive 2 points from each player."

"Give 2 points to each player."

"Lose a turn."

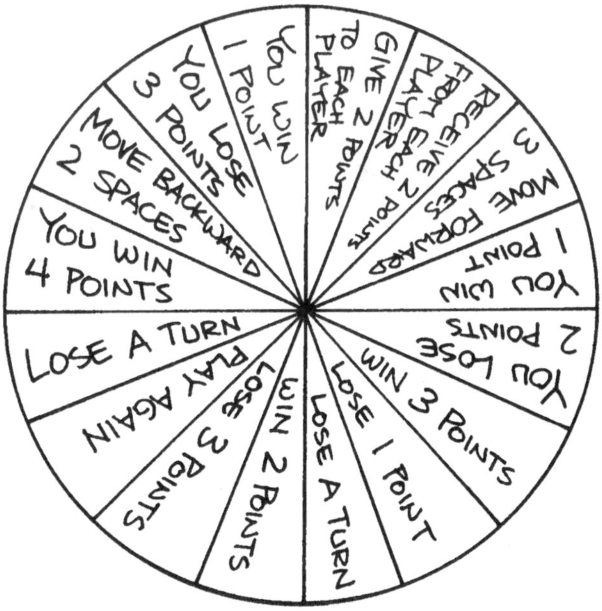

❷ Each player selects a different colored marker or crayon.

❸ Choose one player to go first. Have another player tie the scarf (or bandanna) around the first player's head. With the colored marker or crayon, the first player tries to make a mark on the wheel. It can be an x, a dot, or any other small mark. The player must follow the fortune he or she marks on the wheel. For example, if he or she lands on "you will win one point," he or she wins a point. If the player's mark lands on a spoke, on the wheel rim, or outside the wheel, no points are given.

❹ Each player takes a turn. Between turns, another player should turn the wheel. It's okay if more than one player lands on a fortune. When everyone has had five turns, players add up their points to see who is the winner.

Did you predict the winner?

63 A, E, I, O, U . . . TABOO

What would it be like if there were some letters of the alphabet you couldn't use? You could bet it would make writing a letter difficult and carrying on a conversation a real challenge.

WHAT YOU'LL NEED

- three or more players
- dictionary

HOW TO PLAY

1. For the first round, pick a word leader. The word leader chooses one vowel—a, e, i, o, or u—that can't be used. For the rest of the game, players may not use words that contain that vowel.

2. The word leader asks each player a question, one by one. Each player must answer immediately. No hesitation is allowed or the player will be out of the game. Answers must be longer than three words and must make sense!

3. If there is any disagreement about the spelling of a word, the word leader checks it in the dictionary. The word leader's word is final!

4. Here are some sample questions and correct answers if the taboo vowel is *a*:

Leader:	"Why is science your favorite subject?"
Player 1:	"I like studying the environment."
Leader:	"What will you do on your vacation?"
Player 2:	"I'll hike through the woods."
Leader:	"Why do you like playing baseball?"
Player 3:	"I never strike out."

5. If a player uses a word that contains the taboo vowel, then he or she is out of the game until the next round.

6. The round ends when only one player is left. That player is the winner and becomes the word leader for the next round.

64 EARTH, AIR, FIRE, AND WATER

2

Can you name the correct animal in a set amount of time? Think fast! But be careful, you don't want to be outfoxed.

WHAT YOU'LL NEED

- two or more players
- paper
- pen or pencil

HOW TO PLAY

1. Choose one player to be the caller.

2. The caller starts by pointing to a player and saying one of the following: "earth!" "air!" "fire!" or "water!" Then the caller quickly counts to ten. Before the caller reaches ten, the chosen player must name a living creature that walks on the earth, flies in the air, or swims in the water—depending on the element called. Some examples are fox for earth, bluebird for air, and whale for water. If "fire" is called, the player must remain silent because nothing can live in fire. If the player mistakenly answers with an animal, he or she is out of the game.

3. The caller points to the next player and calls out an element. If an animal has already been used by another player, it can't be used again. The caller keeps track of the animals on a sheet of paper.

4. The caller continues until a player answers incorrectly. That player takes the caller's place for the next game.

65 ROADSIDE SCAVENGER HUNT

Here's a scavenger hunt game you can play without ever leaving the comfort of your car.

WHAT YOU'LL NEED

- two or more players
- paper
- pen or pencil
- watch

HOW TO PLAY

1 Together, make a list of people and objects you are likely to see on your trip. You can make the list as long as you want. Here are some suggestions:

recreational vehicle
silo
farmer
two-color hydrant
spotted cow
tractor
plane
police officer in patrol car
boat on a trailer
billboard with an 800 phone number
license plate with the letter *s*

❷ Now assign either 1 or 2 points to each item. Less common items, such as a family of pigs, can be worth 2 points. Easier-to-spot items should be worth 1 point.

❸ Players can divide up into two teams, or they can play individually. Once you start playing, keep alert. You have thirty minutes to find all the items.

❹ The player who is the first to call out an item on the list initials the "find" with one of his or her player's initials. If two players call out an item at the same time, they both initial it and split the points between them.

❺ The player or team with the most points at the end of thirty minutes is declared scavenger supreme!

66 WORMY BOARD

PARENTAL SUPERVISION REQUIRED

This fun balancing contest is sure to "worm" its way into your list of favorite travel games.

WHAT YOU'LL NEED

- thin twine or string
- tape
- macaroni (small, straight variety)
- medium-weight cardboard (the back of a writing pad works)
- scissors
- ruler
- watch with second hand (optional)

Never use scissors in a moving vehicle, especially a car, bus, or train. Cut out what you need before you leave.

BEFORE YOU LEAVE

1 Make a base for the Wormy Board by marking off and cutting out a 4-inch cardboard square. With a parent's help, use scissors to poke four holes in the 4-inch square. The holes should be about 1 inch from the edge of the board in a square pattern.

2 Now make your "worms." Cut four pieces of string, each about 12 inches long. Wrap a piece of tape around each end to prevent the string from unraveling. This will also make threading your "worms" easier.

3 Bead 3 to 4 inches of macaroni onto each string. Tie a big knot at one end of the string so the macaroni doesn't fall off.

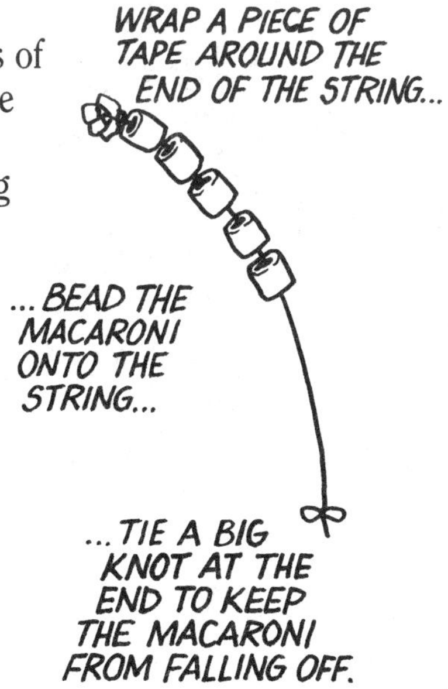

4 Thread the four unknotted ends of the strings through the holes (one string per hole) on the cardboard base. Tie the four strings together in a single knot 3 inches below the board.

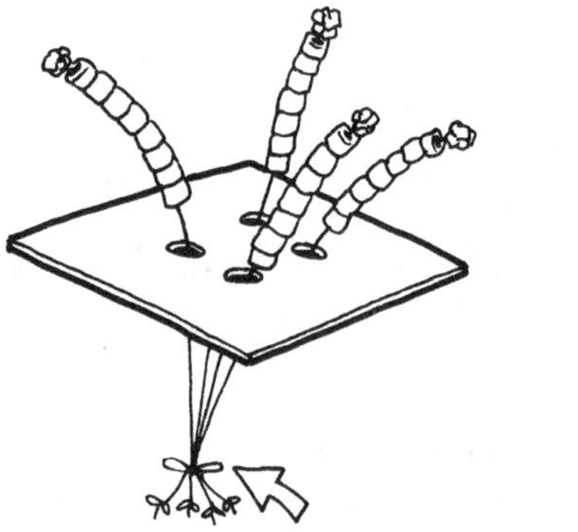

HOW TO PLAY

1 The player holds the board firmly in one hand, then with the other hand pulls on the strings knotted together beneath the board. The object of the game is to shake out the worms first, then tug firmly on the strings, forcing the worms to stand up straight.

2 Let each player take a turn. Play for three rounds, keeping track of who gets the most worms to stand up. The player who gets all four worms to stand up first wins. If you are playing alone, you can time yourself and try to beat your time!

ONE STEP FURTHER

For more of a challenge, try six or eight worms. Or make each worm an inch longer. Just remember to tie your knots tight, or you might have macaroni all over the backseat of the car!

67 DETECT-A-WORD

You and your pals will be ace detectives when you decode clues to hidden words.

WHAT YOU'LL NEED

- two players
- paper
- pen or pencil

HOW TO PLAY

1. Choose one player to go first. Player 1 writes a three- to five-letter word on a piece of paper, then folds the paper in two so that the word cannot be seen. Player 1 announces how many letters are in the hidden word.

2. On a separate piece of paper, Player 2 makes a solving chart. He or she makes two columns, one for the guesses and one for the clues. Each of these columns will have spaces for the number of letters in the hidden word (three lines for a three-letter word, and so on).

3. Now the real detective work begins. Player 2 takes a guess at the word and writes it down in the column under guesses.

4. Player 1 looks over the guess. In the clue column, he or she puts an O in the corresponding space for every correct letter that is also in the correct position, an X for every correct letter that is in a wrong position, and a dash for every incorrect letter.

5. Player 2 now examines the clues and comes up with another answer. The game continues this way until Player 2 guesses the hidden word. Here's an example of how the game would work if the secret word were *trip*:

GUESSES	CLUES
1. city	--X- (*t* is part of the word but not in the correct position.)
2. tear	O--X (*t* is in the correct place, but *r* is not.)
3. trap	OO-O (*t, r,* and *p* are correct.)
4. trip	OOOO (That was easy!)

6. When Player 2 guesses the word, switch places. The player who takes the least number of guesses is the winner.

68 CRAZY NUMBER MAZE

Now you know what you can do with all those old paper cups hanging around. Make your own amazingly easy portable maze.

WHAT YOU'LL NEED

- shoe box top
- ten paper cups
- glue
- marble
- scissors
- watch with a second hand

Never use scissors in a moving vehicle, especially a car, bus, or train. Cut out what you need before you leave.

BEFORE YOU LEAVE

1. Start collecting coffee or soda paper cups. You will need ten cups. Cut an arch into the side of each cup, at the bottom. The arches should be big enough for a marble to roll in and out of. You can shorten the cups, too, so that they are level with the lip of the shoe box top.

2. Glue the cup bottoms to the inside of the shoe box top, and let it dry.

3. Randomly number the cups from one to ten. Consecutive numbers should NOT be next to each other.

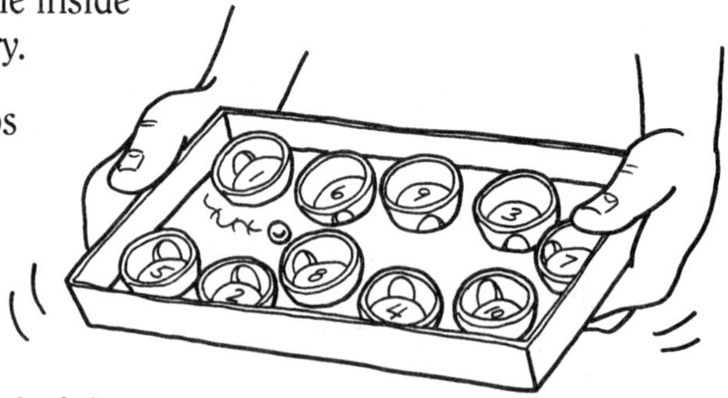

HOW TO PLAY

1. Place the marble on one end of the maze and begin tilting the board back and forth. You have two minutes to roll the ball into all the cups in consecutive order. But be careful. If your marble rolls into the wrong cup, you will have to start over again.

2. The winner is the player who can get the marble into all the cups (or as many as possible) in the allowed time. In case of a tie, play again, but reduce the time to one minute.

69

SALT AND PEPPER

Don't worry, this isn't a cooking recipe. It's a game about things that go together in pairs.

WHAT YOU'LL NEED

- two or more players
- paper
- pen or pencil per player
- watch

HOW TO PLAY

1 Give everyone a piece of paper and a pencil or pen. Tell them to write down as many pairs as they can think of, as long as they are pairs everyone is familiar with. Here are some ideas to get you started:

pots and pans
bread and butter
Batman and Robin
sticks and stones
cops and robbers

2 Set a time limit of five minutes and begin writing down your pairs. When the five minutes is up, compare lists. Each pair equals 1 point. If a player writes down a pair that none of the other players are familiar with, no points are given. The player with the most points is the winner!

70 VANISHING BODY

Don't lose your head . . . or your arm or your leg. In this word game you'll have to work hard *not* to complete words or your body will disappear on you.

WHAT YOU'LL NEED

- two or more players
- piece of paper per player
- pencil with eraser for each player
- dictionary

HOW TO PLAY

1. Everyone grabs a piece of paper and a pencil and draws a simple stick figure using eight parts: a head, a body, two legs, two feet, and two arms. The stick figure is you, and your goal is to keep all of your body parts.

2. Choose one player to go first. The first player calls out a letter to a word he or she has in mind. The second player adds a letter, but tries to add something that will not finish the word, or else he or she loses. For example, if Player 1 calls out "I," then Player 2 says "T," the word is finished (IT). But if Player 2 says "V," the word keeps going (in this case, Player 2 was thinking of the word *IVY*).

3. Players continue to take turns until someone is forced to finish the word. The unlucky player who completes the word has to erase a body part. With each completed word, the player erases a body part, until he or she vanishes—on the paper and from the game.

4. At any time during the game, players have the right to challenge another player's letter if they think the player is making up a word just to avoid finishing another word. The challenged player has to prove the word is correct by looking it up in the dictionary. If a player can't prove it, he or she must erase a body part. But if the player proves the word is real, the challenger loses and must erase a body part.

5. The game continues until all the players but one have vanished! The last player with one or several body parts still existing wins!

71 TRAVEL TREK

The race is on! Who will be the first to get through the treacherous maze and make it home safely?

WHAT YOU'LL NEED

- two players
- pen or pencil for each player
- watch
- 8½-by-11-inch graph paper or 8½-by-11-inch plain paper and ruler for each player

HOW TO PLAY

❶ First each player needs to make his or her own maze. On a piece of graph paper, draw sixty-four squares—eight squares across by eight squares down. If graph paper isn't available, use plain paper and a ruler to make your boxes, each box being about ½ inch.

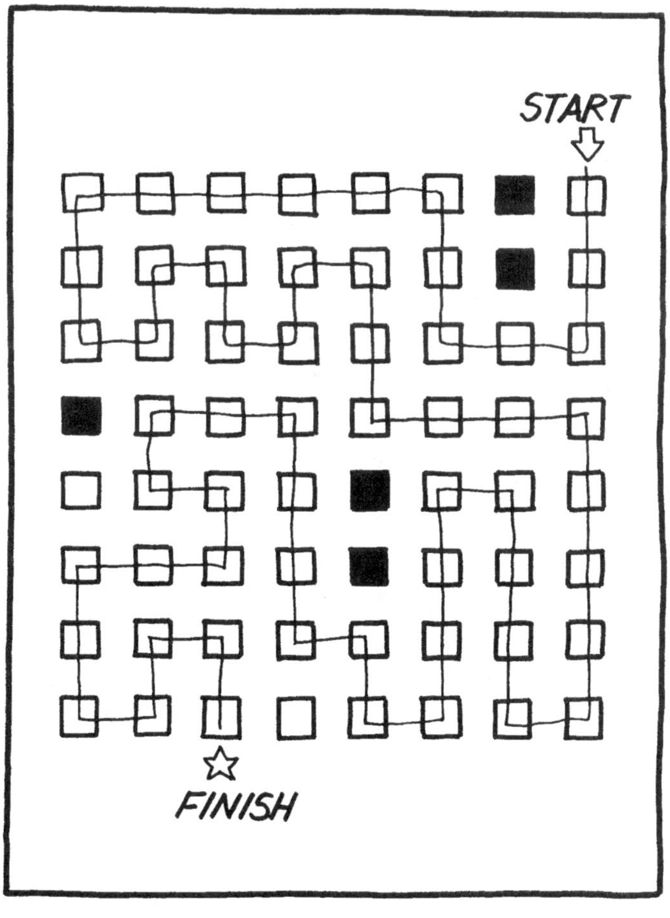

2 Pick any five squares and color them in. You will not be able to pass through these solid blocks.

3 Now pick a start point and a finish point. These can be any of the outside squares. When you are finished making the maze, switch papers with the other player. Each player will use the maze the other player made.

4 Now everyone has one minute to plot a path through the blank squares. You can move horizontally or vertically, but not diagonally. There are only two other rules to remember: 1) You can only go through a blank square once; 2) You must go around the solid squares.

5 When the time is up, count how many blank squares were not passed through. The winner of this game is the player who plots a path "home" through as many of the blank squares as possible. Make a new maze, filling in five new squares, and play again!

72 KING OF THE JUNGLE

What animal do you think is the king of the jungle? A lion? An elephant? In this game, even a lowly rat can claim the crown!

WHAT YOU'LL NEED

- two players
- paper
- pen or pencil
- markers or colored pencils
- cardboard (in two colors)
- scissors
- ruler
- flat surface or lap board
- coin

Never use scissors in a moving vehicle, especially a car, bus, or train. Cut out what you need before you leave.

BEFORE YOU LEAVE

1 Make your jungle game board first. With a ruler, divide the paper into sixty-three squares (eight lines down, ten lines across). With the pen or pencil, fill in the squares on your game board in the following manner:

"Den" = Draw two (one at each end of the board).

"Trap" = Draw six (three around each den).

"Lake" = Draw two. Each lake is six squares. They should be in the center of the board.

The rest of the squares are land within the jungle.

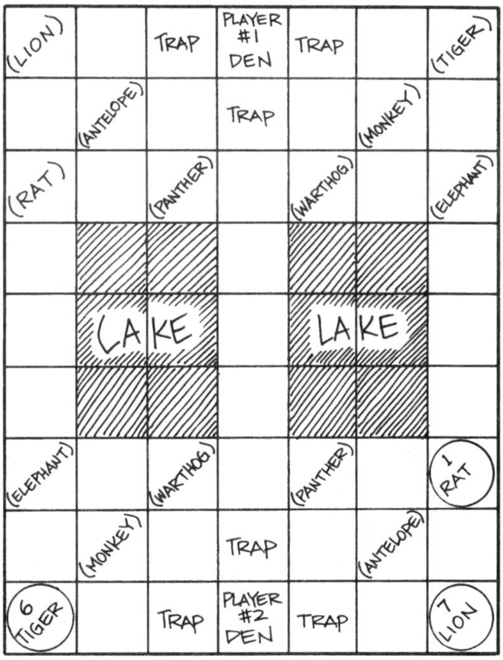

2 Next make your animal game pieces. Cut eight small circles from each of the two colors of cardboard, each circle about 1 inch in diameter.

Each player will have one color, like in the game of checkers. Write in the following numbers and animal names on each set of game pieces:

1 = Rat	2 = Monkey	3 = Warthog	4 = Antelope
5 = Panther	6 = Tiger	7 = Lion	8 = Elephant

The number on each game piece is the value of the animal.

HOW TO PLAY

1. With the game board on a flat surface, set up the animals (game pieces) as shown in the illustration. Flip a coin to see who will go first. The goal of the game is to be the first player to move any animal into an opponent's den.

2. Players take turns moving one animal at a time. Each player moves one of his or her animals into an adjoining square, either down or across. No diagonal movements are allowed. Players can move to any of the empty land squares or onto a square occupied by an opponent's animal to make a capture. In order to capture an opponent's animal, your animal has to be of equal or higher value. For example, an antelope can take another antelope and a lion can take a panther, but a monkey can't capture a warthog. Once an animal is captured, it is removed from the board. An exception to the rule is when a player enters another player's traps. When in an opponent's trap, the animal loses its value. That means any animal can capture it, so keep an alert eye.

3. The water is off limits to all animals, except the rat. That makes the water a safe place for the rat. The tiger and lion are the only animals capable of jumping over the water squares, either vertically or horizontally. That makes them a threat to unsuspecting animals on the other side of the water.

4. The player who gets one of his or her animals into the opponent's den is the winner. As you continue to play, there are a couple of strategy ideas to keep in mind: (1) It's a good idea to keep one or two animals around your three traps; (2) Try to capture as many of your opponent's animals as possible; and (3) Remember, it's not always the strongest animals who survive, but the smartest.

73

HERE TO THERE

When you're done with this game, your spare change will have done as much traveling as you have!

WHAT YOU'LL NEED

- paper
- pen or pencil
- eight pennies
- eight nickels
- flat board or lap desk

HOW TO PLAY

1 First make a game board. On your paper, draw two nine-square boxes (three rows of three boxes) that intersect at one central corner square. (See illustration below).

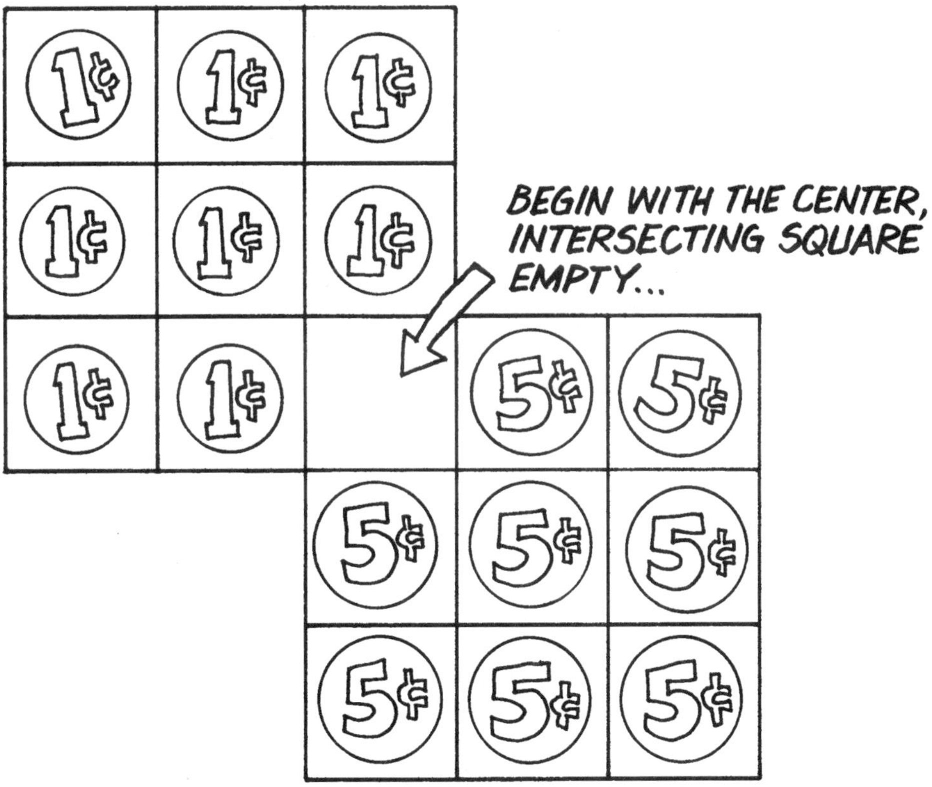

❷ Place eight pennies in the boxes to the left and above the center square, and eight nickels in the boxes to the right and below the center square. Remember to leave the center square empty.

❸ Now start moving your coins. The object of this game is to get the nickels where the pennies are and the pennies where the nickels are. Pennies can only be moved down or to the right. Nickels can only be moved up or to the left. Coins can be moved into an empty square or jump over another coin vertically or horizontally (not diagonally) into an empty square. You don't have to alternate between pennies and nickels. You may move one penny after another penny, for example, as long as you *move*!

❹ One last rule: You must get the coins from here to there in forty-five moves or less! So keep track of each move on the bottom of the page.

74 LICENSE TO PLAY

What's a car trip without a license plate game? Try this one and see if you have the winning hand.

WHAT YOU'LL NEED

- two or more players
- paper for each player
- pen or pencil for each player

HOW TO PLAY

1. Decide which player will go first, second, and so on. As a car passes, the first player writes down the license plate number on a piece of paper. The second player writes down the license plate number of the next car, and so on. If the license plate has more than five numbers on it, use only the first five. Any letters that appear on the license plate have no bearing on the game and should be ignored.

2. Once everyone has written down his or her numbers, each player examines the number to see what combination of numbers he or she has. Certain combinations are worth more than others. Here is a list in the order of their value, beginning with the lowest:

   One pair (two like numbers on one plate)

   Two pair (two sets of two like numbers on one plate)

   Three of a kind (three like numbers on one plate)

   Straight (five numbers in numerical order)

   Full house (three of a kind and two of a kind)

   Four of a kind (four of the same number)

3. All the players lay down their papers to see who has the highest hand. The player with the highest combination wins. If two hands have the same combination, the one with the highest numbers in the combination takes the hand. For example, three fours are higher than three twos.

4. The player who wins the most hands after five rounds earns the license to win.

75 LICENSE PLATE GAME—THE SEQUEL

Movies and books aren't the only entertainment that can have sequels. Here's another variation of the license plate game that you can play alone or with friends.

WHAT YOU'LL NEED

- paper
- pen or pencil
- map
- watch

HOW TO PLAY

1. First you need to assign points to each state, depending on its location in relation to the state you're in. A license plate from the state you are in is worth 0 points. A plate from a neighboring state is worth 1 point. A plate from two states away is worth 2 points, a plate from three states away is 3 points. You'll probably need to refer to your map to figure out the points. If you live in the continental United States, license plates from Alaska and Hawaii are worth an extra 10 points each. Any out-of-country license plates (Mexico, Canada, and beyond) are worth 15 points.

2. Everyone grabs a piece of paper to keep track of his or her own points, then starts watching for passing cars. When a player spots a license plate from another state, he or she yells, "Out of state plate," and points the plate out to the other players to verify the claim. The player then writes his or her points down.

3. Players continue to claim license plates and write down points. Keep in mind that states may be claimed more than once.

4. After thirty minutes, count up the points. Who has the most points?

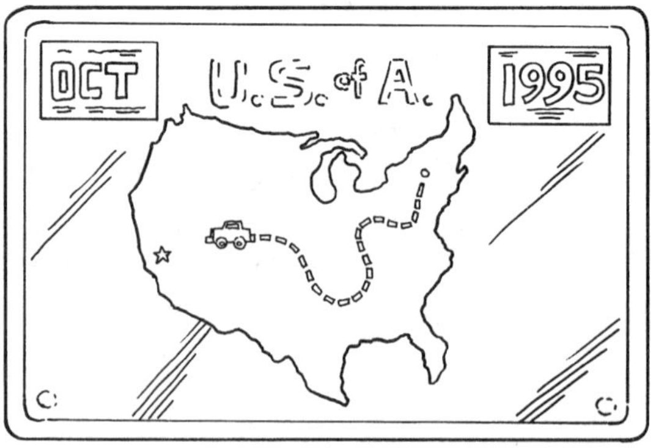

ONE STEP FURTHER

To keep the competition going, even if it's only with yourself, try to name the state capitals of the license plates on your list!

76 RHYME MIME

2

This is a great "acting" out game where using words is out. But that doesn't mean you can't make a funny face or a silly sound!

WHAT YOU'LL NEED

• two or more players

HOW TO PLAY

❶ Choose a player to be "It." "It" picks two words that rhyme—any two words, such as "cat" and "hat." One of these words will be the *game* word. The other will be the *clue* word.

❷ "It" will then say to the other players, "My clue word is 'hat.'" The other players will now know that the game word that they're looking for is a word that rhymes with "hat," in this case, "cat."

❸ Next the players take one turn each acting out their guesses—without, of course, ever saying a word. One player might tap the top of his head for "pat." Another player might puff out her cheeks for "fat." The winning player might meow like a "cat." Players can use sound effects as well as hum the tune to a famous song if it helps to get their guess across. But just remember—no words!

❹ If the guesses are wrong, "It" boos. When the guess is right, "It" cheers. Players get 1 point for every right answer.

❺ Each player gets two tries at guessing it right. If no one gets the right answer, the player who is "It" gets a point. The player who does guess the word is "It" for the next round. Play five rounds, and at the end, the player with the most points wins.

77 COUNTDOWN

During your trip you'll see a lot of numbers—on license plates, billboards, sides of trucks, road signs, and mailboxes. If you can keep track of those numbers, you can play this game!

WHAT YOU'LL NEED

- two or more players
- paper for each player
- pen or pencil for each player

HOW TO PLAY

❶ Keep your eyes peeled and ready to claim numbers. Begin by looking for the number "100." It can be part of another number, such as "1,000," but must be whole. (For instance, "1,010" would not work.) The first player to see the number "100" claims it by calling out, "I see 100." He or she points out the number to the other player(s) to verify it, then writes down the number on a piece of paper.

❷ Next everyone looks for the number "99," then "98," and so on until one player claims every number in order, down to "0." To shorten the game, start from the number "50" or "25."

ONE STEP FURTHER

For a variation of this game, look for numbers in multiples of five (5, 10, 15, and so on) and play to 50 or 100!

78 MYSTERY LETTERS

If you like to draw, this unique spelling word game will suit you "to the letter!"

WHAT YOU'LL NEED

- two or more players
- crayons or markers
- paper for each player

HOW TO PLAY

1. All the players decide on a subject, such as "vehicles." Other categories could be "cartoon characters," "cities," "sports," "games," "zoo animals," "food," and "TV shows."

2. Each player then decides on a four- to ten-letter word that fits in the category. For example, "motorcycle" is a ten-letter word that fits in the "vehicles" category. Keep the word to yourself! On a sheet of paper, each player prints the letters of his or her word in a scattered fashion all over the page—and not in the correct order! The letters should be about 2 inches tall. Don't let the other players see your paper.

3. Now each player makes a drawing that includes these letters as part of the picture. Turn a "B" into a pair of sunglasses. An "I" can be one side of a Greek column. Maybe a "K" is part of a road sign. An "E" can be the bottom of a ladder. Use your crayons or markers to make the drawings as detailed as possible. You want to disguise the letters enough so they can't be easily found. You may not include any letters other than the ones contained in your word.

4. When everyone is finished, switch drawings with the other players. The first player to find the hidden letters and figure out the mystery word wins this game.

79 UGH! A BUG!

Don't scream! No, that's not a huge bug crawling across your paper. It's just part of this fun dice game where players compete to be the first to draw a complete bug.

WHAT YOU'LL NEED

- two or more players
- sheet of paper per person
- pen or pencil per person
- one die (from a pair of dice)
- flat surface or lap desk

HOW TO PLAY

1 First decide in which order players will take turns. Then take turns rolling the die. Each person draws the part of the bug that corresponds to the number he or she rolled on the die. See list below:

1 = body

2 = head

3 = one feeler (two feelers are needed to complete the bug)

4 = an eye (two eyes are needed)

5 = mouth or stinger

6 = one leg (six legs are needed)

2 Continue taking turns rolling the die and adding bug parts until one player has a complete bug.

ONE STEP FURTHER

To make it more challenging, no player can begin drawing the bug parts until he or she has the bug's body. If a one doesn't come up on the die, the player passes the die to the next player. After the body, the bug must have a head, so a two will have to be rolled. After that, the body parts can be placed in any order.

80 NOT ME!

This game starts out slow and simple but quickly picks up speed and difficulty, leaving the losers wondering "why me?"

WHAT YOU'LL NEED

• four or more players

HOW TO PLAY

❶ Pick a player to be the game leader. The leader keeps track of the rest of the players and increases the pace of the game to make it more difficult. The leader assigns each player a different number.

❷ Then the leader starts the game by clapping. While the leader continues to clap, he or she begins the round by calling on one player. That player and the leader exchange six lines while the leader continues to clap. Here's an example:

LEADER: "Number 6."
NUMBER 6: "Not me!"
LEADER: "Why not?"
NUMBER 6: "Don't wanna be!"
LEADER: "Who then?
NUMBER 6: "Number three."

❸ The next player (in this example, Number 3) jumps in to repeat the rhyming verse with the leader.

NUMBER 3: "Not me!"
LEADER: "Why not?"
NUMBER 3: "Don't wanna be!"
And so on.

❹ Players continue to call on each other. Stay alert! Players never know when they will be called upon.

❺ After a few moments, the game leader begins increasing the pace of the game by clapping and calling out in a faster rhythm. With each new verse, the momentum picks up. Players will have to drop out as they forget, repeat, or mix up the verse—and they will! The last player left to answer wins the round and becomes the new leader.

81 PENNY FOR YOUR THOUGHTS

When everyone is taking a nap and there's nothing to do, here's a great game to play alone.

WHAT YOU'LL NEED

- paper
- pen or pencil
- thirty-six pennies
- flat board or lap desk

HOW TO PLAY

1. First, make a game board by drawing thirty-seven circles on a piece of paper. You'll have seven rows: Rows 1 and 7 have three circles; rows 2 and 6 have five circles; rows 3, 4, and 5 have seven circles. To draw your circles, trace around a penny.

2. Now place one penny on each circle, except for the circle in the center of the board. This circle must be unoccupied at the start of the game.

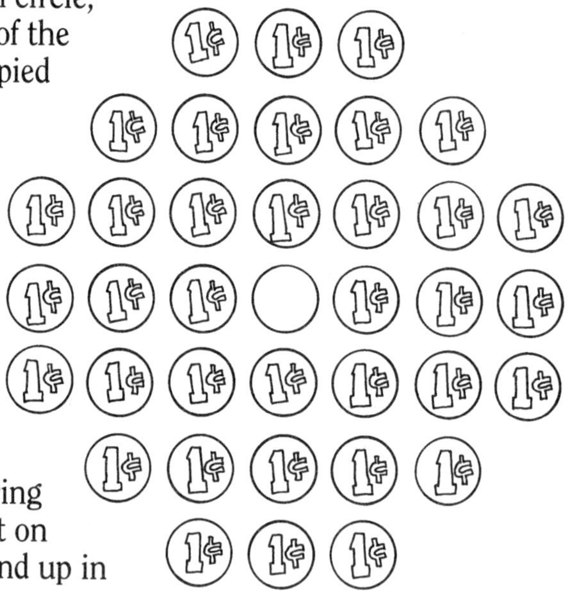

3. The object of the game is to remove pennies one by one by jumping them with other pennies. You can jump horizontally or vertically (no diagonal jumps are allowed). Once you jump over a penny, remove it from the board.

4. Continue jumping and removing pennies until only one penny is left on the board—and that penny must end up in the center circle of the board.

If you don't win the first time, try again. That's the fun of playing against yourself—no one can see your mistakes!

82 CAPTURE!

Have you ever played "capture the flag" with your friends? Here's a version of that game you can play while traveling. But be alert. This three-part game takes strategy, math, and most of all, diplomacy.

WHAT YOU'LL NEED

- two players
- 8½-by-11-inch plain paper
- one black pen or pencil
- colored pens or pencils (one color for each player)
- coin

HOW TO PLAY

PART ONE — MAPPING IT OUT

1. To begin, make a playing map. To do this, players take turns drawing twenty-six make-believe countries on the plain paper using a black pen or pencil. After the first country is drawn, the remaining countries must touch at least one of the other countries.

2. Take turns labeling each country with one letter from the alphabet, eventually using all twenty-six letters (each letter can be used only once). The countries do not have to be labeled in alphabetical order.

3. Now each player picks a different colored pen or pencil. This way you know which player occupies which countries. Each player writes down his or her name and the number "100" in a corner of the board. This is the number of troops each player starts with. Now the strategy begins.

PART TWO — THE OCCUPATION

4. Flip a coin to decide the order of play. Player 1 picks a country he or she wishes to occupy and writes down the number of troops he or she will station in that country. If Player 1 wants to put eight troops inside Country C, then he or she would write eight inside that country. Now Player 1 subtracts eight from his or her total troops of one hundred. (This is the number under your initials in the corner of the paper.) Players will keep a running tally of their own troops.

5. The players take turns deploying their troops until all the countries have been occupied and all the troops stationed. (With twenty-six countries, each player will end up with thirteen countries apiece.)

PART THREE — THE CAPTURE

6 Now comes the exciting part—attacking and capturing as many of your opponent's countries as possible. Player 1 decides which country he or she wants to capture first. The country has to be touching one of Player 1's countries.

7 Player 1 can attack with one or more countries, as long as the attacking countries are next to the country under attack. The total of the combined troops has to be greater than the total troops in the country being attacked. For example, Player 1 has troops in three countries (Q, S, and Z) surrounding Player 2's Country R. The combined total of the three countries' troops is eight, five more than Country R's three troops.

8 Once a player captures a country, it is colored in his or her color. This means the captured country, and the troops within, are out of the game. The conquering troops can be used again.

9 Players take turns (only one capture per turn) until no other country can be captured. The player with the most captured countries is the winner.

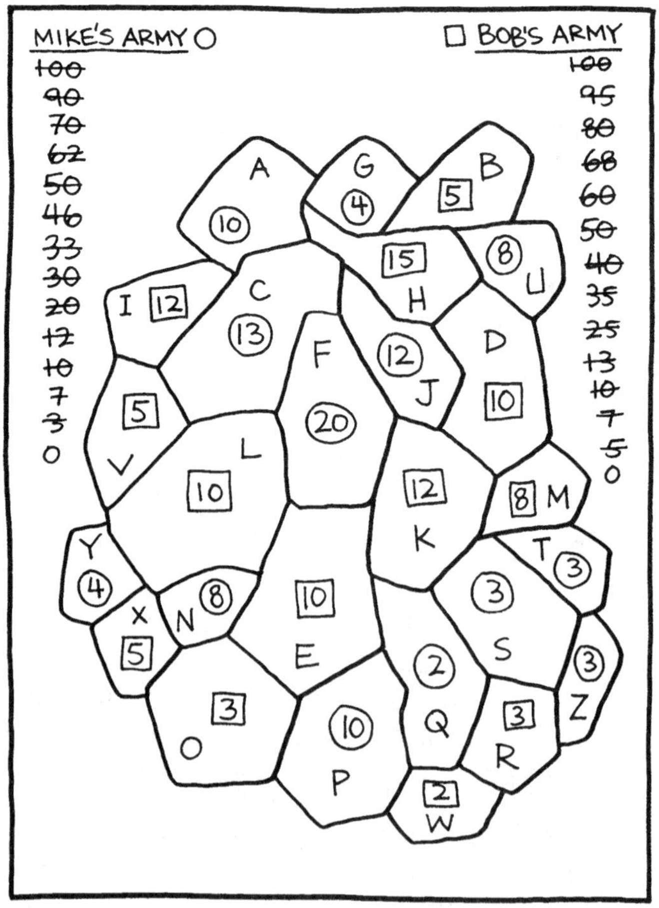

83 I "NOSE" IT

You know where your nose is, or your knee, right? Well, in this silly mix-up game what you say may not be what you mean!

WHAT YOU'LL NEED

• two or more players

HOW TO PLAY

1. To begin, the first player points to a part of his or her body and calls it a different body part. For example, a player might point to his or her knee and say, "This is my *nose*." The player then quickly counts to five.

2. Before the first player reaches five, the next player must point to the body part the previous player named and call it something else. So, using the previous example, the player would point to his or her *nose* and call it something else, like a *finger.*

3. As you continue to play, increase the pace. Someone is bound to get mixed up. Each time someone says the wrong body part, he or she is eliminated from the game. The last player left is the winner!

84 ALWAYS A WINNER

Here's a game you can't lose. That is, until your opponent learns the secret!

WHAT YOU'LL NEED

- two players
- flat board or lap desk
- twenty-one pennies (or other small objects)

HOW TO PLAY

1. Place the twenty-one pennies on a hard surface in any order you wish. Tell your opponent that you will take turns removing one to three pennies at a time. The player who removes the last penny is the loser.

2. Now, here's the secret for a sure win each time—your opponent must go first. He or she will think you're being nice, but actually you're being tricky! If your opponent draws one penny, you draw three. If he or she draws two, you draw two. Whatever your opponent draws, you draw enough pennies to total four for that round.

3. Start playing, taking turns removing pennies following this strategy. After five rounds you will have removed twenty pennies. That leaves one penny left for the sixth round. When your opponent goes first, he or she will have to pick it up!

85 TAC-TAC-CAPTURE

Is tic-tac-toe losing its challenge for you? Here's a version that's bound to keep you on your toes!

WHAT YOU'LL NEED

- two players
- pen or pencil for each player
- 8½-by-11-inch plain paper and ruler or 8½-by-11-inch graph paper

HOW TO PLAY

1. First you will need a game board. If you have graph paper, skip to the next step. Otherwise draw a large box on a plain piece of paper. Use a ruler to draw lines on your paper, twelve rows across by twenty rows down. Lines should be about ½ inch apart.

2. Decide who will be "X" and who will be "O." Choose one player to go first. The first player starts by placing his or her mark in one of the squares. The second player follows by placing his or her mark in another box. The goal of the game is to capture your opponent's mark by surrounding him on all four sides with your mark. (Diagonal corners don't count.)

3. Players continue to mark squares until one player captures another player's mark. That player then draws a box around the captured square.

4. Continue playing until all the squares are filled. The player who has the most captured marks is the winner.

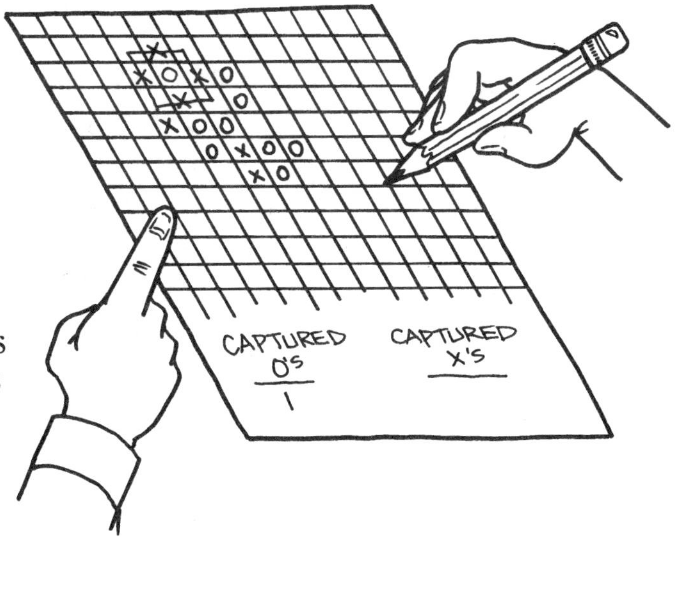

86 MY ADORABLE, BASHFUL CAT

1

Cats! You either love them or hate them. But you always have something to say about them. In this game, players take turns describing a cat. Easy? Guess again!

WHAT YOU'LL NEED

- two or more players

HOW TO PLAY

1. The first player chooses a word to describe a cat that starts with an *a*. For example, "My cat is an adorable cat."

2. The second player must repeat the *a* word as well as add a *b* word to describe the cat, such as "My cat is an adorable, bashful cat."

3. The next player adds a *c* word. For example, "My cat is an adorable, bashful, carefree cat."

4. The players continue taking turns, repeating all the descriptions for the cat and coming up with a new word that begins with the next letter in the alphabet. If you forget any of the words, get them out of order, or can't come up with a new word—sorry, you're out of the game! If you can keep the cat's description going, you can win the game! Now, *that's* the cat's meow!

87 OLD MAC'S CRIBBAGE

Cribbage is a game you may have seen your parents play using a deck of cards and a special cribbage board. All you need for this travel version is a good pair of eyes and a paper and pencil.

WHAT YOU'LL NEED

- two players (or two teams of players)
- pencil or pen per player
- paper per player

HOW TO PLAY

1. Each player (or team) looks out one side of the car looking for objects from the list in Step 2. They can only count the items spotted on their side of the car.

2. When a player sees an item, he or she calls out that object. For example, "I have a red barn." The first player then writes down the item on a piece of paper and receives a certain number of points based on a prearranged list such as the one below. (You may add to this list as you wish.)

   1 point = a farm animal (no more than five at one time)
   2 points = a red barn
   2 points = a tractor
   2 points = a pair of dogs
   3 points = three dogs together

If you pass a cemetery on your side of the car, all your points are wiped out and you must begin again.

3. Players continue searching for objects and writing down points. The first player to reach 121 points wins.

88 SIGN HUNT

Before you sign out of your trip, you've got to try this road-sign game that will provide you with loads of signed, sealed, and delivered amusement.

WHAT YOU'LL NEED

- two or more players
- paper for each player
- pen or pencil per player
- watch

HOW TO PLAY

1. The object of this game is to spot as many road signs as possible in ten minutes.

2. Players begin by scouring the countryside for signs.

3. All road signs count: speed signs, warning signs, city signs, service signs, construction signs, and so on. Only billboards don't count.

4. The first person to see a sign claims it by calling out the name of the sign. For example, "That stop sign is mine!" Once a player has spotted and claimed a sign, no other player can use it.

5. Players continue to claim signs, each keeping track of how many they see on a piece of paper. At the end of ten minutes, players count up the signs they have found. Each sign is worth 5 points. The player with the most points wins.

89 SPELL BOUND

Can you spell W-I-N-N-E-R? That's what you'll be once you master this spelling game.

WHAT YOU'LL NEED

- two or more players
- 8½-by-11-inch plain paper
- pen or pencil
- lunch-size paper bag
- dictionary

HOW TO PLAY

1. Have one person tear a piece of paper into thirty-one small pieces. Write each letter of the alphabet (A through Z) on each piece of paper. On the remaining five pieces, repeat each of the vowels (A, E, I, O, U). If there are four or more players, make another set of the alphabet and vowels for a total of sixty-two pieces.

2. Put all the letters into the paper bag and give it a shake.

3. Each player draws one letter from the bag to determine the order of play. The player who draws the letter nearest the end of the alphabet will be first.

4. Everyone puts those letters back in the bag, and the first player then draws five letters from the bag and lays them face up. That player now tries to make a word using at least three letters. If the player makes a word, he or she gets 5 points.

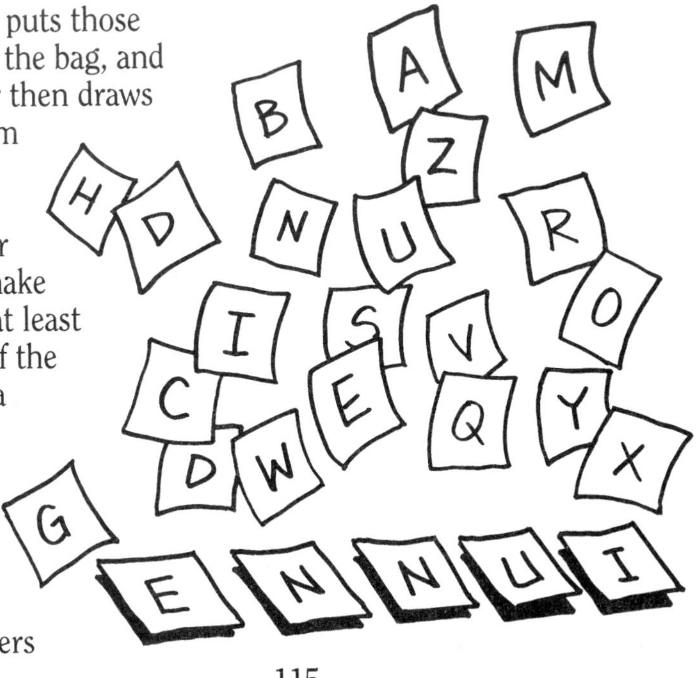

5. The next player draws five letters

and tries to make a word with them. Once everyone has had a turn, each player takes turns drawing one letter at a time. Players can use the new letters in combinations with other letters they have to make a word or to add onto a word they've already made. For example, adding an "e" to "mad" makes "made." Because this is considered a new word, the player receives 5 points for this as well.

6 At any point in the game, a player can ask another player for one of his or her letters instead of taking one from the bag.

7 If at any time a player suspects another player of making up a word, he or she can challenge that player and look up the word in the dictionary. If a challenged word is not in the dictionary, the player who used the word loses 5 points and the challenger gains 10 points. If it is in the dictionary, the challenger loses 10 points.

8 Players continue to draw letters and make words, keeping track of their points. When no other words can be made from the remaining letters, players total up their points to see who wins.

90 FLY ON THE WALL

Have you heard the expression "a fly on the wall"? Well, what if you were a fly in the car? Do you think anyone could find you if you didn't want them to?

WHAT YOU'LL NEED

- two or more players
- paper
- pen or pencil

HOW TO PLAY

1. The first player thinks of a specific place in the car to hide if he or she were as small as a fly. The player then writes it down on a piece of paper. Be as detailed as possible. For example, instead of writing "in the backseat," write "between the backseat and the center seat belt." This will make the game more fun and challenging.

2. Each player makes a guess as to the "fly's" hiding place. He or she would say something like, "If I were a fly, I would hide behind the visor" (or wherever else he or she thinks the fly is hiding). The first player, or "fly," responds by buzzing. The closer the guessing player is to the hiding place, the louder the "fly" buzzes.

3. When one of the players guesses the location correctly, the "fly" buzzes three times quickly. But remember, guesses have to be exactly as written on the paper. The first player to guess correctly gets to be the next "fly on the wall."

91 LEAVE A MESSAGE

2

How many times have you taken a phone message for someone and gotten it wrong? Well, here's a chance to redeem yourself.

WHAT YOU'LL NEED

- two or more players
- paper for each player
- pen or pencil per player

HOW TO PLAY

1. Choose a playing order. Each player takes a turn calling out one letter of the alphabet—any letter. (You can also use a letter more than once.) Keep saying letters until you've called out ten letters.

2. Then each player composes a phone message using words beginning with the letters in the order they were called out. The message can be funny, but it should make sense (a sort of off-the-wall sense, at least). For example: *W-P-F-B-W-I-Y-M-P-S = William, please find Bobby's weasel inside your mother's pink sweater.*

3. Each player takes turns reading his or her message. There are no winners or losers here. The idea is to come up with the coolest messages.

ONE STEP FURTHER

Instead of choosing random letters, use the letters in a name, a type of car, or a city you're traveling through. For example: *Kalamazoo = Kind archaeologist lost Aunt Margie at zoo only once.*

92 CHANGE THE ENDING!

How many times have you read a book or watched a television show and been disappointed with the ending? Here's your chance to finish the story the way you want!

WHAT YOU'LL NEED

- two or more players
- paper for each player
- pen or pencil per player

HOW TO PLAY

1. Choose a player to go first. One player begins by telling a short version of his or her favorite short story aloud. Try sharing a fairy tale such as "The Three Little Pigs" or maybe your favorite Power Rangers episode! Tell the beginning of the story in one or two sentences, then the middle section of the story in another two or three sentences. Then stop before you get to the end.

2. Now everyone else writes down a new ending and takes turns reading it aloud. Didn't you always want the wolf to win out just once over the last little pig? Or, have the bad guys beat the Power Rangers? Go ahead. It's your story now.

3. Once all the players have written their endings, take turns reading them aloud. Vote on the best ending, the funniest ending, or the scariest ending.

93 FRANKY'S FRIEND

1

A leg here, a head there. Throw in an arm or two. Dr. Frankenstein isn't the only one who can create a monster. So grab a couple of friends and create your own monsters.

WHAT YOU'LL NEED

- three players
- paper
- markers or crayons

HOW TO PLAY

1. Have a person fold a piece of paper into three parts, like an accordion.

2. The first player draws a head on the top section of the paper without letting the others see. It can be anything from a pig to a pygmy, a senator, or a centipede. Then the player folds the paper over so that the blank middle section is showing and hands it to the second player.

3. The second player draws the body, without letting the other players see and without peeking at the head. When the second player is finished, the player folds the paper so that the blank bottom portion of the paper is showing and hands it to the third player.

4. Now the third player adds the legs and feet. Again, no peeking at the head or body.

5. Finally, when the three drawings are complete, unfold the paper to reveal your creature. Now create a whole village of creatures to keep Franky's friend company!

94 GUESS WHO?

2

Have you ever wished you could change places with your favorite actor or sports star? Well, stop dreaming and start talking!

WHAT YOU'LL NEED

- three or more players

HOW TO PLAY

❶ Two players choose a pair of famous people each will play. They can be anyone, from famous people to historical figures to fictional characters. But they should be characters whom the other players would recognize. Have fun and choose two characters who belong together, such as Fred Flintstone and Barney Rubble, or two characters who have something in common, like Abraham Lincoln and Bill Clinton.

❷ To start the game, the two players have a conversation in character in front of the other players. Here are some subjects they might talk about:

Favorite foods?

Family? (Are you married? Do you have children?)

Where were you born?

What's your favorite mode of transportation?

❸ The other players listen to the conversation and try to pick up clues. No questions are allowed.

❹ If one player figures out who the characters are, he or she doesn't shout out the answers. Instead, the player joins in the conversation as another character who would know them. For example, Wilma would certainly have something to say to Fred or Barney. And, Abe and Bill would have lots to talk about with George Washington. As the other players guess who the characters are, they too can join the conversation. There are no winners, but everyone is sure to have something to talk about.

95 STUFF IT

If the backseat of the car is getting littered with used paper cups and straws, don't despair. And don't throw them out!

WHAT YOU'LL NEED

- two or more players
- paper cup with lid
- straws (one for each player)
- toothpicks (ten for each player)
- watch with second hand

HOW TO PLAY

1. Search the backseat and find yourself a paper cup with a tight-fitting lid. You'll also need one straw for each player and ten toothpicks.

2. Stuff the straws through the center hole in the lid. If the hole isn't big enough, push your fingers through it to enlarge it. Now bend, twist, and make small tears in the straws.

3. Taking turns, each player picks a straw and has one minute to work as many toothpicks down the straw as possible. Since the straws are misshapen, this can be rather difficult. You may have to use one toothpick to push down another. Or, hold the straw away from the bottom of the cup so that the toothpicks can pass through the straw and into the cup. But hurry, the clock is ticking.

4. Whoever is left with the least number of toothpicks in his or her hand is the winner.

96 THROUGH THE WINDOW

2

PARENTAL SUPERVISION REQUIRED

What if you locked yourself out of the car, and your favorite music cassette was inside, melting in the hot sun? In this game there's only one way to get inside and get your things . . . through the windows!

WHAT YOU'LL NEED

- 10-inch-square cardboard
- markers or crayons
- knitting needle or scissors
- yarn, 5 feet long
- scarf for blindfold

Never use scissors in a moving vehicle, especially a car, bus, or train. Cut out what you need before you leave.

BEFORE YOU LEAVE

1. On your cardboard, draw a side view of a car (or a van or truck). Make sure it has one or two doors, two windows, a trunk, and an engine hood. Now color the car with your crayons or markers making it as simple or elaborate as you want.

2. Using the knitting needle or scissors, have a parent randomly punch several holes all over the cardboard, both on the car and outside of the car. Make sure there are two or three holes punched into each of the doors and windows and the hood and trunk of your vehicle.

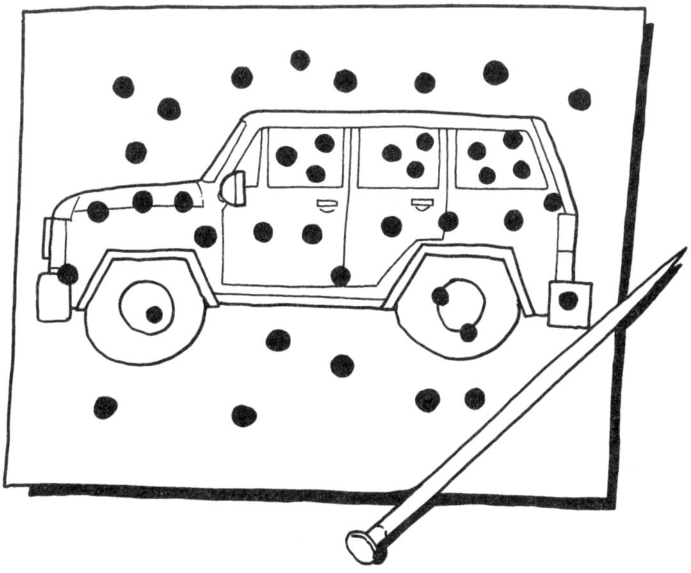

HOW TO PLAY

❶ Choose a player to go first. The first player is blindfolded and given a 5-foot length of yarn. Another player places the cardboard car in front of the player, turning it a couple of times. The player threads the yarn through as many holes as possible, then takes off the blindfold.

❷ The player receives 2 points for each hole within a window, and 1 point each for the car hood and trunk. If the player pokes through the blank area of the cardboard, he or she loses 2 points. And if the player threads through the door, he or she loses all of his or her points.

❸ Let the other player have a chance to crawl through the car window. Then add up the points. The player with the most points wins!

97 WRONG WAY DEFINITIONS

Do you have the time for a little rhyme? See if you can keep up with this rhyming and definition game.

WHAT YOU'LL NEED

- two or more players
- paper
- pen or pencil

HOW TO PLAY

1. This game is more fun with a lot of players. Get Mom and Dad involved. There is no keeping score and no set playing order. Just jump in when you think of a new rhyming word.

2. One player starts the game by giving a word and a definition. But the definition he or she says is for a word that *rhymes* with the given word. Say the word you choose is "bear." Don't give the definition "a big, furry animal." Instead, say something like this: "A bear is a place where a wolf sleeps." The word you are defining is "lair," so the second player might respond: "Don't you mean *lair,* which is what you do when you look at something too long?" (Here, the word is "stare.")

3. The object of the game is to keep the rhyming and misdefinitions going for as long as possible. Try to come up with a word that has a lot of rhyming words. The more words, the longer you can keep the game going. Here are a few rhyming words to get you started:

   bear, fair, hair, footwear, Delaware, mohair, stair, pear, snare, square, tear, share, care, rare

   pet, fret, jet, fishnet, Corvette, cadet, wet, vet, sweat, sunset

   blast, cast, passed, mast, past, forecast, last, mast, broadcast, aghast, harassed

4. When no one can think of any more rhyming words, pick another word and start again.

98 THE CLOCK STRUCK

1

If your little brother and sister are getting restless, try this fun game to help them "kill time."

WHAT YOU'LL NEED

- two or more players
- piece of paper per player
- pencil

HOW TO PLAY

1. Each player is given a piece of paper and told to draw the face of a clock. The clock should fill most of the page. Draw the numbers on the clock, but don't include the hands.

2. The first player closes his or her eyes. While this player's eyes are closed, the other players turn the first player's paper clock around and around.

3. The first player then waves the pencil over the paper and recites the nursery rhyme:

Hickory dickory dock,
The mouse ran up the clock,
The clock struck . . .

4. After the line "The clock struck," the player drops the pencil point onto the clock. Now the player can open his or her eyes. One of the other players then crosses out the number the pencil is on, or nearest to. If the number is already crossed out, the player loses his or her turn.

5. The other players take their turns. Players continue taking turns until someone marks off all the numbers on his or her clock. That person is the winner . . . for the time being!

99 HONEYCOMB

Save up straws from snack stops and make a honeycomb. Don't worry. This game isn't sticky unless you forget to wash the soda off the straws!

WHAT YOU'LL NEED

- two or more players
- scissors
- construction paper
- tape
- twenty to thirty straws

Never use scissors in a moving vehicle, especially a car, bus, or train. Cut out what you need before you leave.

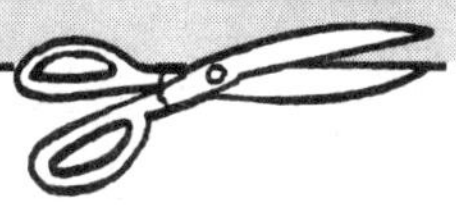

BEFORE YOU LEAVE

Cut the straws you've collected into three different lengths—short, medium, and long. There should be an equal number of straws for each size.

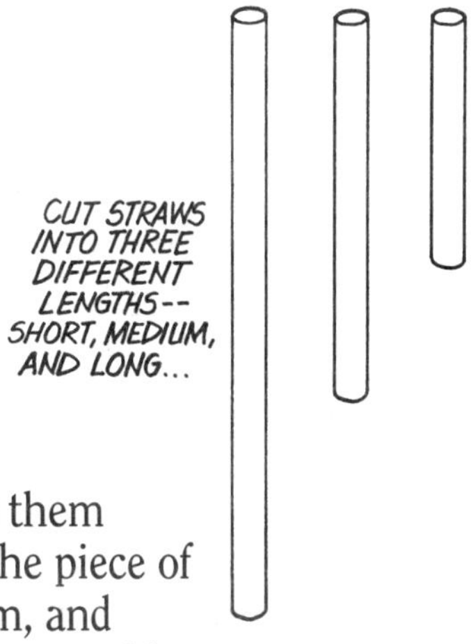

HOW TO PLAY

1. One person gathers straws together and places them inside a paper cylinder made by rolling and taping the piece of construction paper. The short, medium, and long ends of the straws should be covered by the paper. Make sure the paper is tight. Now tap one end of the straws on a hard surface. Notice how the ends of the straws look like a bee's honeycomb?

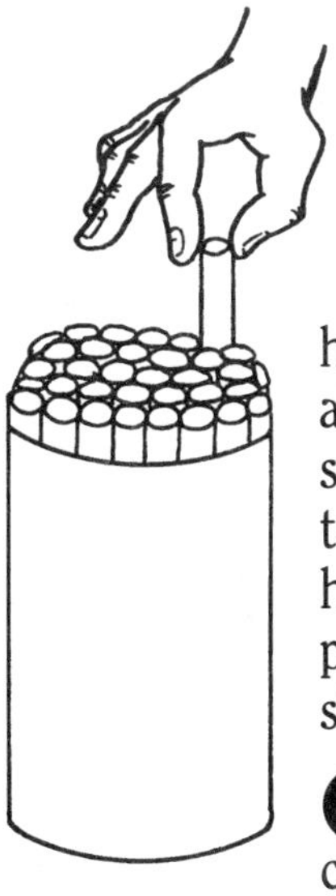

2. To play, take turns pulling straws out of the honeycomb. But stop after you've pulled the straw out about 1 inch. At this point you must declare whether the straw is short, medium, or long. If you guess right, you get to keep the straw. If not, put the straw back into the honeycomb. The next player then makes a choice. If that player can remember where the replaced straw is, he or she can pull it out.

3. After everyone has had five turns at the honeycomb, count straws. In a tie, count who has the most long straws.

100 THE TRAVELIN' ALL-STAR FAMILY BAND

1

Here's another way to put the garbage littering the backseat to good use. Make rhythm instruments and start your own band!

WHAT YOU'LL NEED

- empty soda cups
- empty yogurt containers
- plastic lids
- hard candies
- rubber bands

HOW TO PLAY

1. You can make your own rhythm instruments with just a few empty containers that you find in the backseat. Anything you can shake, rub, blow, or beat will work. Use your imagination! Here are a few ideas:

   Drums: Empty soda cups and yogurt containers with plastic lids help keep a beat.

   Maracas: Put several hard candies inside a cup and replace the lid. Now shake it up.

   String instruments: Use a rubber band stretched around a large cup for that twangy sound.

   Horns: Blow into an empty candy box. You've heard of a French horn. Well, this is a duck horn. At least that's what you will sound like.

2. Now pick a tune everyone knows and strike up the band!

CARD TRICKS

INTRODUCTION

Before you shuffle up some fun, here are a few things you need to know:

BOOK: A group of four cards that have the same value is known as a book. Four sevens are a book of sevens; four tens are a book of tens.

CARDS: There are fifty-two cards in a regular deck. These cards are divided into four different suits: clubs, spades, hearts, and diamonds. There are thirteen cards in each suit. The cards, in order from high to low, are ace, king, queen, jack, ten, nine, eight, seven, six, five, four, three, and two.

DEAL and DEALER: To deal means to pass out the correct number of cards to each player. A dealer normally passes out one card at a time, face down, around the circle clockwise, then deals to himself or herself last. After each hand, the next player in the circle becomes the dealer, so everyone gets a chance to deal.

FACE CARD: Face cards have a picture of a person on them. The face cards are the king, queen, and jack.

FACE UP or FACE DOWN: This is an instruction for how to deal or play the cards. Face up means that the front of the cards show. Face down means that the back design of the cards show.

HAND: The cards dealt to you in a game are called a hand.

PAIR: Any two cards that share the same number or face card are a pair, such as the two of hearts and the two of diamonds, or the queen of spades and the queen of diamonds.

WILD CARD: This special card beats the high card in a game. The wild card varies, depending on the game.

101

SLAP HAPPY

Who has the quickest reflexes? Find out in this fast-moving game that really *jacks* up the fun!

WHAT YOU'LL NEED

- two to six players
- paper to keep score on
- pen or pencil

HOW TO PLAY

1. Choose one person to be the dealer. The dealer shuffles the cards and deals out the entire deck, one at a time, face down, to the players.

2. Players pick up their cards but don't look at them.

3. When the dealer says "go," all players turn the top card from their stacks face up into the middle of the circle.

4. Players check the cards quickly. If there is no jack, the dealer says "go" again. Everyone turns over another card. Continue playing until someone turns over a jack.

5. As soon as you spot a jack, slap your hands twice over your head, then slap the jack. The first player to slap the jack gets to pick up all the cards in the middle and set them face down in a pile in front of him or her.

6. Keep playing until all four jacks in the deck have appeared. The player who slaps the last jack not only gets the middle cards but also collects all the cards from the other players' stacks.

7. Players count up the number of cards they've won. The dealer writes down the scores on a piece of paper. The person with the highest score at the end of three games is the winner.

102 COLOR CHANGE-O

Amaze and astound your friends into believing you can change the color of the cards in a deck by simply blowing on them.

WHAT YOU'LL NEED

• deck of cards with a joker

HOW TO DO IT

1 In order to make the trick work, prepare your cards in advance when no one is looking. Arrange the entire deck of cards in alternating colors: one red, one black, one red, one black, and so on. Place each black card about ¼ inch below the top of each red card. Now place the joker on top so no one will be able to see the final black card. Turn the deck over so that the back design is showing.

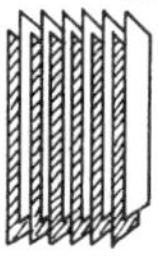

2 Find a friend or family member to be your audience. You are now ready to demonstrate your trick.

3 Tell your audience, "First, let me show you the deck. It is entirely made out of red cards." Carefully grip the bottom of the cards in your right hand, so no one will see that the cards are staggered. Firmly run your left thumb through the tops of the cards, and only the red cards will show.

4 Now say to your audience, "I can change the color of these cards simply by blowing on them." Turn the cards upside down, and grasp the bottom of the deck by your left hand. Blow on the deck of cards. Then firmly run your right thumb through the tops of the cards, and only the black cards show.

5 For the grand finale, tell your audience, "Now I will mix up the colors of the cards simply by blowing on them." First, quickly tap the cards with your fingers. This will make all the cards line up together and mix up the colors. Then blow on the deck for effect. Flip through the stack with your thumb, and the colors will now be mixed, red and black together!

103 GO FISH

2

Hook up pairs of cards in this game that's even more fun than fishing. The best part is you won't have to touch any worms!

WHAT YOU'LL NEED

• two to five players

HOW TO PLAY

❶ Choose one person to be the dealer. Before the dealer shuffles, he or she removes one card from the middle of the deck and sets it aside without looking at it. This is called the "shark." The dealer then shuffles the cards and passes out seven cards to each player, one at a time, face down.

❷ The dealer next places the leftover cards face down in a stack in the center of the circle. These cards are called the "fishpond." The dealer then takes one card from the fishpond and places it face up next to the fishpond. This is the throw-away pile.

❸ Players hold their cards in a fan shape and arrange them by pairs.

❹ Players remove any pairs from their hands and place them face down in front of them.

❺ The person to the left of the dealer goes first. He or she goes on a "fishing expedition" to find cards that will make pairs with the cards in his or her hand. To do this, he or she asks one of the other players for a needed card. For example, if the first player has a six and wants to make a pair, he or she asks any one person of his or her choice, "Do you have any sixes?" If that player does, he or she has to give it to the first player. The first player then lays down the pair face down in front of him or her and continues asking other players for cards until he or she can't make a pair. If the player asked doesn't have the card requested, he or she says, "Go fish." The first player must then go to the fishpond, take the top card, and add it to his or her hand.

❻ If the card from the pond allows the player to make a pair, the player continues asking other players for cards, until he or she can't make a pair.

❼ At any time during his or her turn, if a player has a card he or she can't find a pair for, he or she can say, "I think I have the matching shark." Remember, the shark card was the one card the dealer laid aside in the beginning of the game. The dealer turns over the shark, and if the player is right, he or she wins the game! But if the player is wrong, he or she loses a turn.

❽ Then, the next player "goes fishing." Players keep taking turns until someone is completely out of cards. Everyone counts his or her pairs. The player with the most pairs is the winner. If all the cards in the fishpond are used before someone runs out of cards, the dealer turns the throw-away pile over, shuffles the cards, and starts a new fishpond with them.

104

WILD ROAR

This is the purr-fect game to bring out your animal instincts!

WHAT YOU'LL NEED

- four to six players

HOW TO PLAY

1. Each player picks an animal and imitates its sound, such as a lion roaring, a dog barking, or a cat purring.

2. Choose one person to be the dealer. The dealer shuffles the cards and deals out the entire deck, one at a time, face down, to the players.

3. Players pick up their stacks of cards but don't look at them.

4. The player to the left of the dealer goes first and turns face up his or her top card, placing it in front of him or her. One by one, each player around the circle also turns up a card and places it in front of him or her.

5. Players keep turning cards onto their own face-up stack until there is a pair. The first player to notice the pair AND make the sound of his or her animal wins both stacks of cards belonging to the two players with the pair. The winner places the two stacks under his or her playing stack.

6. Play until one person has all the cards. He or she is the winner. If you want to end the game before someone has all the cards, have each player count up his or her cards. The player with the most cards wins.

TO MAKE IT TOUGHER: Change the rules so that when a player notices a pair of cards on the table, he or she has to make the animal sounds of both players who played those cards.

105 BOTTOMS UP!

Your friends will never get to the bottom of this easy but impressive trick!

WHAT YOU'LL NEED

- deck of regular playing cards with a picture on the back that has a top and a bottom

HOW TO DO IT

1 Arrange the entire deck of cards so all the tops point in the same direction.

2 Next, approach an unsuspecting friend or family member and tell him or her you can guess what card he or she picks out of the deck.

3 Position the cards in your hand so the bottom of the design is pointing toward your body. Arrange the cards into the shape of a fan, and allow your friend to choose one card and look at it without showing you what it is.

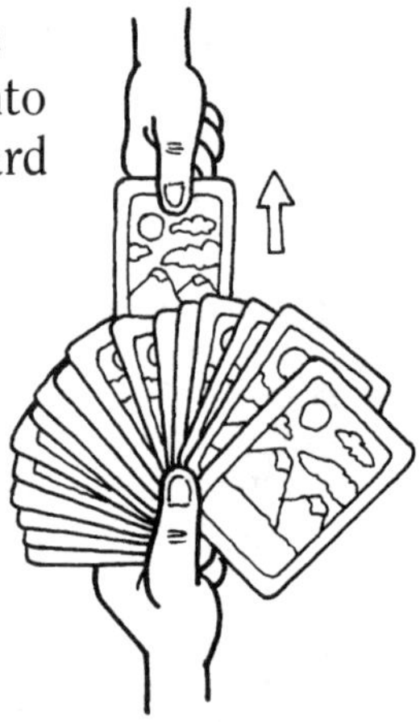

4 While your friend is looking at the card, casually de-fan the cards and turn the pack around so that the top of the design is now pointing toward your body. Ask your friend to replace the card into the middle of the deck. This card will now be the only one with an upside-down back design.

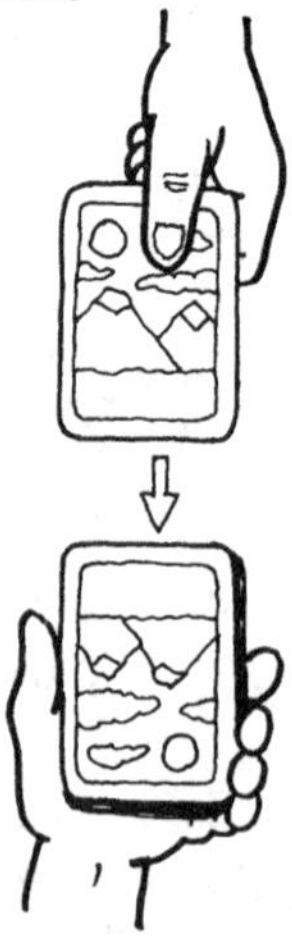

5 Then flip through the cards one at a time. Tell your friend that the chosen card gives off certain vibes that only you can feel. Actually, you are looking for the one upside-down card. When you find it, pull it out and show it to your friend. He or she will be amazed at what a "card" you are at magic tricks!

106 BLACK-ON-RED SOLITAIRE

This twist on the traditional game of solitaire is guaranteed to bring you hours of solo fun.

HOW TO PLAY

1 Sit at a table with enough room to spread out your cards. Then shuffle the cards.

2 First, set up the cards. Start by laying out a horizontal line of seven cards in front of you. Put the first six cards FACE DOWN, from left to right. Turn the seventh, or last card, FACE UP. Cover the first line of cards, starting from the left, with five cards FACE DOWN. Turn the sixth card FACE UP. Cover this line of cards, again starting from the left, with four cards FACE DOWN. Turn the fifth card FACE UP. Cover this line of cards with three cards FACE DOWN. Turn the fourth card FACE UP. Cover this line of cards with two cards FACE DOWN. Turn the third card FACE UP. Cover this line of cards with one card FACE DOWN and one card FACE UP. And finally, on the left-hand stack place a single card FACE UP. Set aside the rest of the cards. You will use them later.

3 The object of the game is to move the cards from this line to four separate piles, in order, from the highest card (ace), to the lowest card (two), alternating colors (black and red).

4 To start, if any aces are showing, remove them and place each one separately above the row. If possible, place any face-up cards on aces above, starting with the king, alternating black and red. Otherwise, to uncover more face-down cards, play the face-up cards on each other by moving higher cards to lower cards, alternating black and red. For example, move a black nine to a red eight, and a red jack to a black ten. Following this rule, move as many cards as possible, each time turning up the next face-down card and trying to play those cards as well. If you turn over an ace, put the ace above. If you turn over a king, place it on the appropriate ace (black on red or red on black).

5 When you can move no other cards, pick up the stack of leftover cards. Count out three cards and turn them face up. If you can play the top card, do so. Then you're free to play the second or third card if possible. When you have no more plays, turn up three more cards and repeat.

6 Move up lines of cards to the aces as soon as you can. Keep playing and moving cards until you have moved all the cards possible from the line up to the new stacks of aces, with the cards all in order, alternating black and red.

7 If you move all of the cards from the line to their appropriate place on the ace stacks, you win. If you aren't able to move all of your cards, play again and see if the second time's a charm!

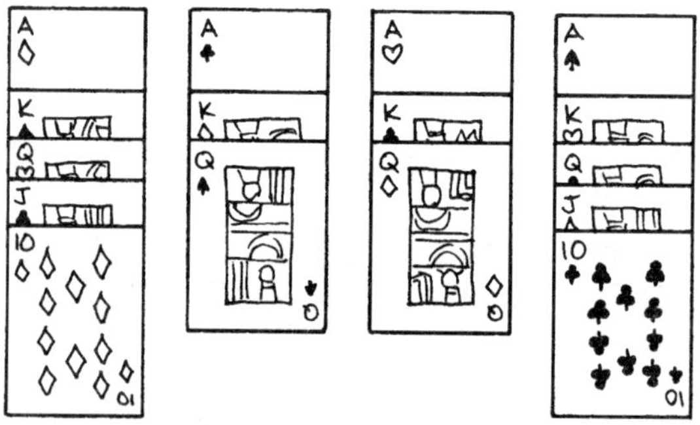

107 IT TAKES A THIEF

Here's a game where you can steal your opponents' cards right out from under their noses!

WHAT YOU'LL NEED

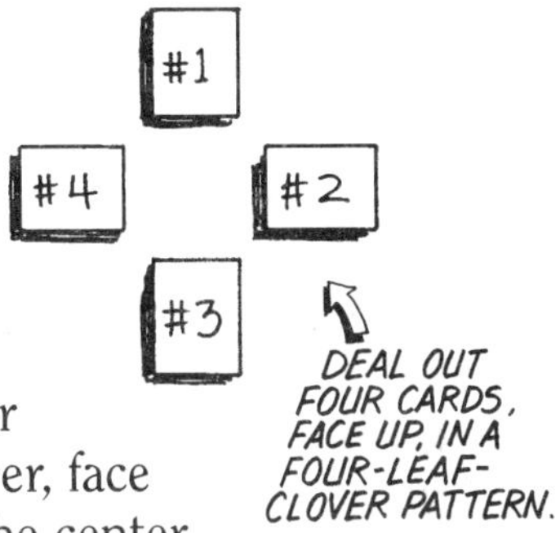

- two to four players

HOW TO PLAY

1 Choose one person to be the dealer. The dealer shuffles the cards and deals four cards to each player, face down. Next, he or she deals four cards face up in the center, in a four-leaf-clover pattern. Each card in the center is called a bundle.

2 The person sitting to the left of the dealer goes first. If that player has a card in his or her hand that makes a pair with the top card of any bundle, the player takes the card from his or her hand and places it on the bundle face up. The player then picks up the bundle and places it in front of him or her with the top card facing up. This is called "stealing" a bundle. The object of the game is to steal as many bundles as possible. If the player can't match a bundle, he or she must choose a card from his or her hand to discard.

3 Now it's the next player's turn to try to match a bundle. He or she can either match and steal a bundle in the center or match and steal another player's bundle. However, if there are fewer than four bundles on the table at any time, the player must use his or her turn to place a card in the empty space, creating a new bundle. There must always be four bundles in the middle of the table.

4 Go around the circle, with each player trying to steal a bundle. When players run out of cards in their hand, they ask the dealer to give them four more cards from the unused stack and continue playing.

5 After all the cards have been played, the game is over. Players count their cards. The player with the most cards wins.

108 STACK THEM UP!

This impressive card trick really stacks the deck in your favor, and it works every time!

HOW TO DO IT

1 With your audience watching, lay out twenty-one cards, face up, into three stacks, one card at a time to each stack. Overlap the cards so your audience can see all seven cards in each stack. Set the rest of the deck aside—you don't need it.

2 Ask a volunteer in your audience to mentally choose any card from one of the stacks and remember it. Next, ask your friend which stack the card is in. Tell the friend, "Just by knowing which stack the chosen card is in, I will find it."

3 Pile the stacks on top of each other so that the stack containing the selected card is in between the other two stacks.

4 Lay the cards out again, face up, into three stacks of seven. Ask the volunteer to again tell you which stack the card is in.

5 Restack the cards, placing the selected stack in the middle between the other two stacks, and again lay them out in the same manner as Step 1.

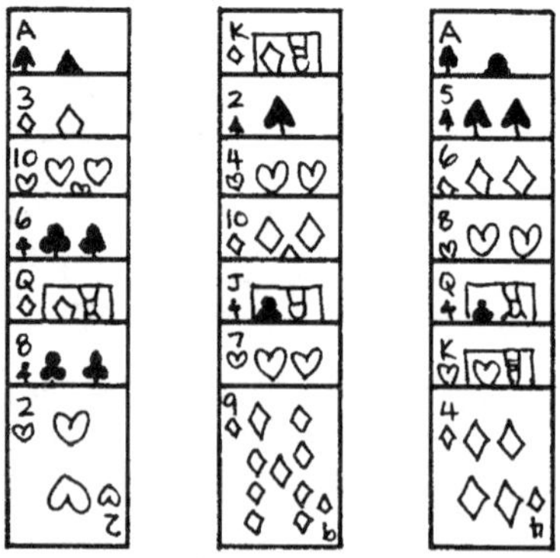

6 Ask the volunteer to tell you for the last time which stack the chosen card is in. Because of the way you laid out and stacked the cards, the chosen card will be the fourth (or middle) card in the stack the volunteer pointed to. Pull out the card and show it to your volunteer. Who is more surprised at your magician's skill—you or your audience?

109 MAID FOR A DAY

2

Old Maid like you've never seen her before! Play it with your family, and make a deal that the loser has to do all of the chores for a day!

WHAT YOU'LL NEED

• two to six players

HOW TO PLAY

1 Choose one person to be the dealer. Ask the dealer to remove the queen of clubs from the deck, because you won't be needing it. The dealer then shuffles the cards and deals them all out, one at a time, face down, to the players. (It doesn't matter if a player or two has one card more than the others.)

2 Players check their cards to see if they have any pairs of the same color—for example, a three of hearts and a three of diamonds. Each player removes all same-color pairs and places them face down in front of him or her.

3 The player to the left of the dealer goes first by arranging his or her cards in a fan shape so they can't be seen by the other players. This player then offers the cards to the player on the left.

4 That player picks one card out of the first player's hand and places it into his or her own hand. If this card makes a same-color pair, the player removes it and places it face down in front of him or her.

5 That player then offers his or her hand to the next player around the circle. That player picks a card and removes any same-color pairs.

6 Players continue going around the circle, picking cards from each other's hands, until all the cards are paired up, except for one, the queen of spades. The person left holding the queen of spades loses, and is "maid for the day"!

STRATEGY ALERT: If you get the queen of spades, play it cool and don't give it away by sighing or rolling your eyes. The game is a lot more fun when no one knows who has the deadly queen.

110 THE VANISHING CARD

Your audience will never disappear on you while you demonstrate this exciting trick that makes a card vanish before their very eyes.

WHAT YOU'LL NEED

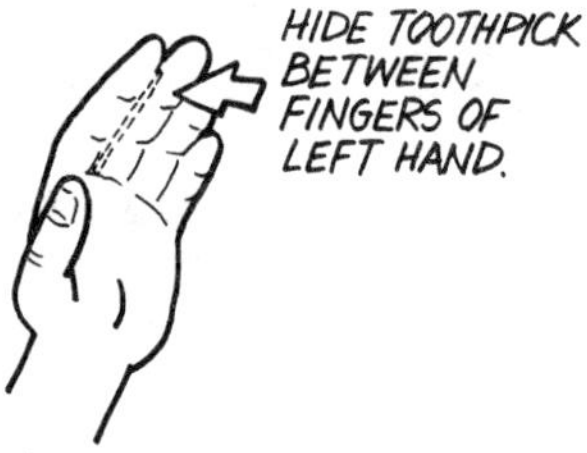

- handkerchief
- regular wooden toothpick

HOW TO DO IT

1 Before you begin this trick, put the toothpick between your index and middle fingers in your left hand so it can't be seen. Place the handkerchief on the table.

2 Put the deck of cards into a pile on a table in front of your audience. With your right hand, pick up the handkerchief and shake it out to show there is nothing inside.

3 Reach for the pile of cards with your left hand. Throw the handkerchief over your left hand. Tell your audience that you will lift up one card *inside* the handkerchief.

4 Instead of picking up a card, roll the toothpick off your fingers and into the top of the handkerchief with your left hand. With your right hand, grasp the toothpick between your thumb and forefinger, and slowly lift the handkerchief up from the table. The toothpick inside the handkerchief will look as if you are holding a card. Wave your left hand over the handkerchief and say, "Abracadabra!"

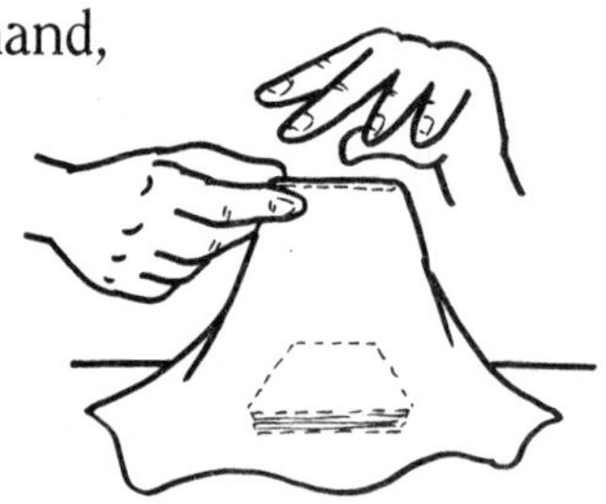

5 With your thumb and fingers of your left hand, grab a bottom corner of the handkerchief and yank it across your body to the left. At the same time, let go of the toothpick. If you do this quickly, and with a large, sweeping movement, no one will notice the toothpick as it drops onto the floor. It will look as if you made the card disappear in thin air!

STRATEGY ALERT: This trick may work better for you if you switch your left and right hands in the instructions above.

111 THE SECRET SPOILER

This card game is the best secret in town—share it with your friends!

WHAT YOU'LL NEED

- two to six players
- extra deck of regular playing cards

HOW TO PLAY

1. Choose one person to be the dealer. The dealer shuffles the cards and deals out the entire deck, one at a time, to the players. (Each player should have the same number of cards. Leftover cards can be set aside for that hand, then reshuffled into the deck for the next hand.)

2. Players arrange their cards by suits. Before play begins, the dealer pulls one card from the middle of the extra deck of cards and sets it aside without looking at it. No one else should look at it either. This card is called the "secret spoiler."

3. The player to the left of the dealer goes first by laying any card of his or her choice into the middle of the circle. Whatever suit the first player puts down is called the leading suit. The other players must play cards from the leading suit. If they don't have one, they can play any other card.

4. The highest card in the leading suit wins the cards for that round. That player picks up the cards and places them face down in front of him or her.

5. Once all the cards have been played, the dealer turns up the secret spoiler card. Now all the players look through their cards and pull out any that match the *suit* or *number* of the secret spoiler.

6. Each player counts one point for each suit that matches the spoiler card and ten points for each number that matches the spoiler card. The person with the *highest* number of points *loses*. You can play from 50 to 500, whatever you have time for.

112 SWITCH-ER-OO

Here's a switch for you—in this game, the ace is low instead of being high. Winners keep playing while losers drop out, until there is only one person left.

WHAT YOU'LL NEED

• six to ten players

HOW TO PLAY

❶ Choose one person to be the dealer. The dealer shuffles the cards and deals one card face down to each player. Players look at their cards.

❷ The player to the left of the dealer goes first. He or she has a choice to either keep the card if the card seems high (kings are the highest) or get a new one if it's on the low side (aces are the lowest). To change cards, the player says, "Switch-er-oo." The player on his or her *right* must switch cards with the first player, unless he or she is holding the highest card, a king. That player must show the king to all the players in order to keep it.

❸ Continue around the circle, with each player taking a turn deciding whether to keep or switch cards.

❹ After everyone has had a turn, all players lay down their cards, face up, in the center at the same time. The person with the lowest card must drop out of this game (remember, aces are low). If two or more players have the same low card, this is considered a tie, and no one drops out.

❺ The dealer collects the cards from the middle and sets them aside, then deals another round of cards to the remaining players.

❻ Continue playing until only one player is left in the game. He or she is the winner. If you run out of cards before there is a winner, the dealer may shuffle the used cards and start again.

113 SPELLBINDING

In this trick, you use an index card to help spell out a friend's chosen card. Can you spell C-O-O-L T-R-I-C-K?

WHAT YOU'LL NEED

- pencil or pen
- 3-by-5-inch index card
- scissors

HOW TO DO IT

1 Use the scissors to cut the index card so that it is ½ inch smaller than a card from your deck. Set this aside until later.

2 Grab a friend from the audience. Explain that in this trick you're going to magically be able to find a certain card in the deck that only the friend has seen.

3 Next, pick up the deck of cards, saying you want to make sure there are no jokers in this deck. This will give you a chance to go through the cards without your friend knowing what you're doing. Turn the deck of cards over so the cards are face up. As you look through the cards, count the cards until you reach the twelfth card. Don't let your friend know you're counting. Remember the number and face of this twelfth card. Put the cards down.

4 Tell your friend that before he or she chooses a card, you're going to make a prediction about which card he or she will choose. Take the index card and tell your friend you're writing down your prediction. But instead write, "THIS MUST BE IT." Don't let your friend see what you've written.

5 Pick up the deck and fan the cards until you see the twelfth card. Put the index card behind the twelfth card, making it the thirteenth card. Don't let your friend see that you're counting cards; simply tell him or her, "Now I will put this index card randomly back in the deck."

6 Square up the deck and place it face down, so that the thirteen cards are now on the bottom.

7 Hand the deck to your friend. Ask him or her to pick up a stack of cards from the top of the deck. Tell him or her to pick up *less* than half the deck.

8 Tell your friend to shuffle these cards and to look at the top card and remember it. Then tell him or her to put the card back on top of the deck and give the deck a cut. Again, he or she should pick up less than half of the deck.

9 Take the deck and cut it at the index card. This will be easy, because the index card is not the same size as the playing cards.

10 Set the top stack to one side and place the bottom stack on top. The index card will be on top of the deck. Because of the way you laid out the cards and cut the cards, your friend's remembered card will now be the twelfth card from the top.

11 Give your friend the index card and ask him or her to read it out loud, letter by letter: T-H-I-S M-U-S-T B-E I-T. Tell your friend, "I will turn over one card for each letter you read, plus one for good luck. The last card I turn over will be the card you remembered." Turn over twelve cards, one for each letter. The thirteenth card will be your friend's chosen card, just as you predicted!

114 CARD-INGO

You'll be calling out for more when you play this card version of bingo!

WHAT YOU'LL NEED

- three to six players
- second deck of regular playing cards

HOW TO PLAY

❶ Choose one player to act as the dealer. This person will not play the game. The dealer then shuffles the cards and deals seven cards, one at a time, face up, to each player.

❷ Players lay their cards face up on the table in front of them, so all of the cards are showing.

❸ The dealer takes the second deck of cards and turns over one card at a time, calling out the number and suit. If a player's card matches the card called out, the player turns his or her card face down. The first person to turn over all cards yells out, "Card-ingo!" and wins the game.

STRATEGY ALERT: Be sure to pay attention to the dealer. If you don't hear a card when it is called, you're not allowed to ask the dealer to call it again.

115 SEVEN UP

2

This game where you build on sevens to get rid of all of your cards will put you in seventh heaven!

WHAT YOU'LL NEED

- three to eight players

HOW TO PLAY

1. Choose someone to be the dealer. The dealer shuffles the cards and deals out the entire deck, one at a time, face down, to the players. (It doesn't matter if a player or two has one card more than the others.)

2. Players look at their hands and arrange the cards in the shape of a fan.

3. The first card played must be a seven. The player to the left of the dealer goes first. If that player is holding a seven, he or she lays it in the center of the table. If that player doesn't have a seven, he or she must pass, and the next person in the circle gets a chance to play a seven.

4. Once the first seven has been played, the next player can build on that seven by adding a card that is higher or lower in the same suit. For example, if the next player has a six in the same suit, he or she places the six to the left of the seven so the cards overlap. If the player has an eight, he or she places the eight to the right of the seven. Or, if the person has another seven, he or she starts a new line by placing it above or below the first seven. If the player doesn't have a card that can be played, he or she passes.

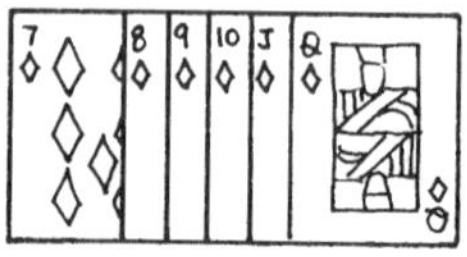

5. The next player takes a turn. Continue around the circle, with each player taking a turn building on any of the cards, adding one higher or lower card in the same suit.

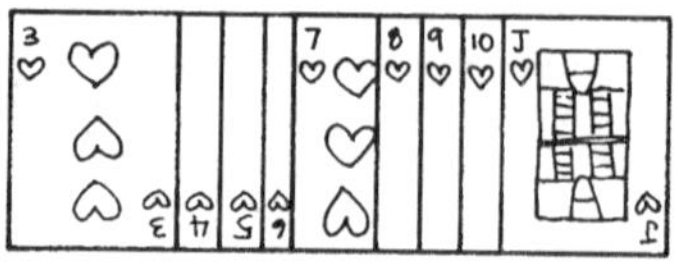

6. Keep playing until one player is out of cards. That player is the winner!

116 DROP AND SNATCH

This trick where you appear to grab a preselected card out of midair will make you look like an old hand at card tricks.

WHAT YOU'LL NEED

- roll of double-sided clear tape

HOW TO DO IT

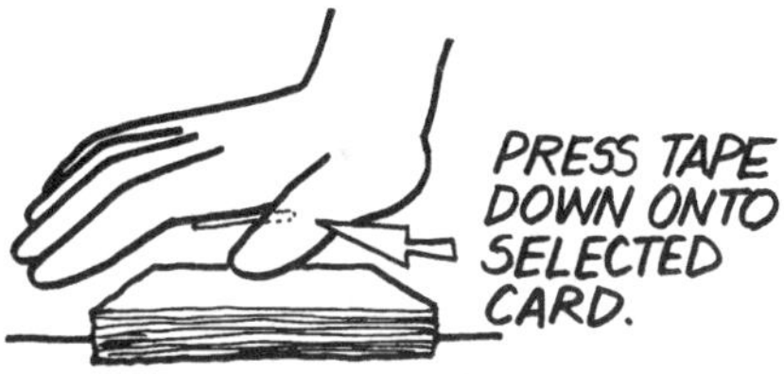

1 When no one is looking, slip a small piece of double-sided tape into the palm of your right hand. Set the deck of cards on the table in front of you, face down. With your left hand, pull a card from the middle of the deck and show it to your audience. Make sure everyone knows which card this is.

2 Place this card on top of the deck. Use your right hand (with the tape) to pick up the top half of the deck, and move it to your right. Keep your right hand over the top of these cards.

3 Now tell your audience, "In a few seconds, I will pluck this chosen card out of midair." Pick up the left stack of cards with your left hand, and throw the cards up into the air. While your audience is distracted by the thrown cards, press your right hand down onto the top card, sticking it to the tape and to your hand. Quickly bring your right hand up and appear to snatch the card out of midair. Show the card around so everyone gets a chance to see it.

117 HEART ATTACK

You'll be more than happy to give your heart away in this classic game of hearts!

WHAT YOU'LL NEED

• two to six players

HOW TO PLAY

1 Choose one person to be the dealer. The dealer shuffles the cards and deals out the entire deck, one at a time, face down, to the players. (Each player should have the same number of cards. Leftover cards can be set aside for that hand, then reshuffled into the deck for the next hand.) Players pick up their cards and arrange them in a fan shape in their hands.

2 The goal of this game is to win as few hearts as possible. The player to the left of the dealer plays first. He or she lays down one card and places it in the middle playing area. All other players follow in order, playing a card from their hand that matches the suit. If a player doesn't have a card in that suit, he or she *must* play a heart. If that player has neither a heart nor a card in that suit, he or she can play any card. The person with the highest card *in the suit originally played* wins the cards in that round, called a trick, and stacks them in front of him or her.

3 The person to the left of the first player begins the second round, laying down a card from his or her hand, with other players following suit. Again, the person with the highest card *in the suit originally played* at the beginning of the second round wins that hand.

4 Continue playing until all the cards have been played. Then players count up how many heart cards they have in their tricks. The person with the least number of hearts is the winner.

STRATEGY ALERT: Because the goal of the game is to win as few hearts as possible, try to avoid playing high cards in the leading suit whenever hearts are played. Also, get rid of any high hearts you're holding by playing them whenever you can't match the starting player's suit.

118

FACE CARD FACE-OFF

Use the kings, queens, and jacks to help you find a chosen card.

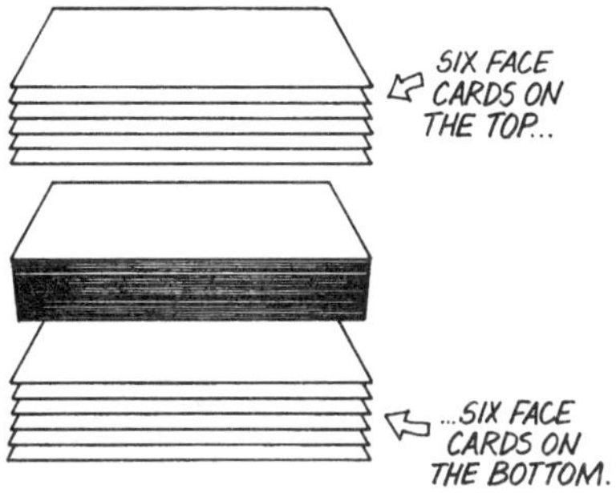

HOW TO DO IT

1 To make the trick work, you'll need to set up the cards in a certain way when no one is looking. First, remove all the face cards—the kings, queens, and jacks. Place six face cards face down on the bottom of the deck and six face cards face down on the top of the deck. It doesn't matter in which order you put them. Next, remove four cards from the middle of the deck—it doesn't matter which ones—and put them aside. For this trick to work, the deck must have only forty-eight cards.

2 Now grab an audience. Lay out the forty-eight cards into six equal piles, face down, one card at a time to each pile. Because of the way you set up the deck, every pile will have a *face card* on the top and a *face card* on the bottom. You don't have to check, they'll just be there.

3 Tell your audience, "I'm going to leave the room. While I'm gone, someone pick a stack and remove a card from the middle of that stack. When you have all seen the card, place it face down on top of the pile it came from. Restack the cards in any order you wish." Then leave the room for a few minutes.

4 When you return, tell your audience, "Now I will find the card you just selected." Look through the deck until you find one *regular* card *in between* two face cards. This is the selected card. Take it out and proudly show it to your admiring audience.

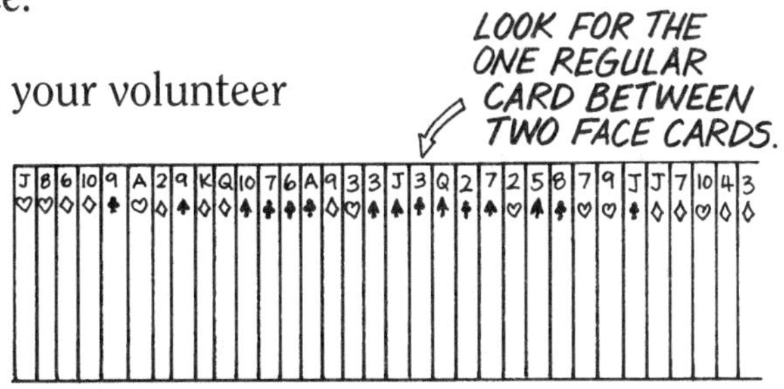

SECRET TO THE TRICK: When your volunteer took a card from a stack, he or she replaced it on the top of the same stack—on top of a face card. And, when he or she stacked the piles together, the bottom card of the stack that went on top was also a face card, thus "surrounding" the chosen card.

119 "THAT'S NOT SO, JOE!"

2

This game is for players who can bluff their way out of anything—even a bad hand!

WHAT YOU'LL NEED

- four to five players

HOW TO PLAY

1. Choose one person to be the dealer. The dealer shuffles the cards and deals out the entire deck, one by one, face down, to the players. (It doesn't matter if a player or two has one card more than the others.) Players arrange their cards in a fan, keeping them hidden from the other players.

2. The goal of this game is to get rid of all of your cards as quickly as possible, in order from the highest to the lowest. The player to the left of the dealer goes first, by removing any aces from his or her hand and putting them face down in the middle of the playing area. The player must also announce how many aces he or she is putting down. If the player doesn't have any aces, he or she can do one of two things: (1) pass or (2) bluff and try to get rid of cards by putting down ones that aren't aces. If, however, another player suspects the first player is bluffing, he or she says, "That's not so, Joe." The first player must then turn over the cards and reveal if they are aces or not. If the player was bluffing, he or she has to pick up the "bluffing" cards and put them back in his or her hand. If the player was telling the truth, the other player has to pick up all the cards.

3. If no one accuses the first player of bluffing, then all the other players discard their aces (if they have any) onto the top of the pile. Only the first player in each round can bluff.

4. In the second round, everyone removes any kings from his or her hand. The first player to put down kings has the choice to bluff or not. In the third round, queens are removed, then jacks, tens, and so on, until all the cards, down to the twos, have been played.

5. If no player has managed to get rid of all of his or her cards, players start back with aces and continue playing until one person is out of cards. This person is the winner. If you have to stop the game before one person is out of cards, have each player count up his or her stack of cards. The person with the least number of cards is the winner.

120 RAISE THE ROOF

Do you have the gentle touch it takes to build a delicate house of cards? Find out in this true test of skill that lays the foundation for many hours of fun.

WHAT YOU'LL NEED

- one to four players
- table with a large, flat surface

HOW TO PLAY

1. The first person takes two cards and turns them lengthwise. He or she places them on a table and pushes them together to make a corner, holding the cards steady until they balance against each other. The player then carefully removes his or her hands. The two cards will stand on their own.

2. The next player adds two more cards, forming a square.

3. Players continue to take turns, adding two cards at a time. Players can either make new squares or lay two cards on top of a square to create a roof. Once a roof is made, players can add another square, or "second story," on the roof.

4. Continue taking turns until one player crashes all or part of the house. Then pick up all the cards, and start building again.

5. The first player to crash the house three times is the loser.

STRATEGY NOTE: Be patient. It can take a few tries before you get the hang of building card houses. But with a little practice, you'll find yourselves getting better and better and building larger and larger structures.

121 ON EDGE

Your friends will stand back in awe when you make an ordinary card stand up on end by itself!

HOW TO DO IT

1. Grab an audience. Take the top card off the pack of playing cards and place it vertically in your hand.

2. While doing this, keep a little conversation going with your audience. Say something like: "This card is the most amazing card in the deck. It can do a very special trick. It can stand all on its own." Then pretend to talk to the card, saying, "Are you ready, card? Everyone is watching you." You only want to talk long enough to get the interest of your audience and to give you some time to set up the trick.

3. While talking, give the card a good squeeze so that the sides slightly bend forward toward each other. The bend will be so slight that no one will probably notice it.

4. Set the bottom of the card on a table and balance it. The slight bend you've given the card is just enough to keep the card standing. Gently pull your hand away. Voilà! It works just like magic!

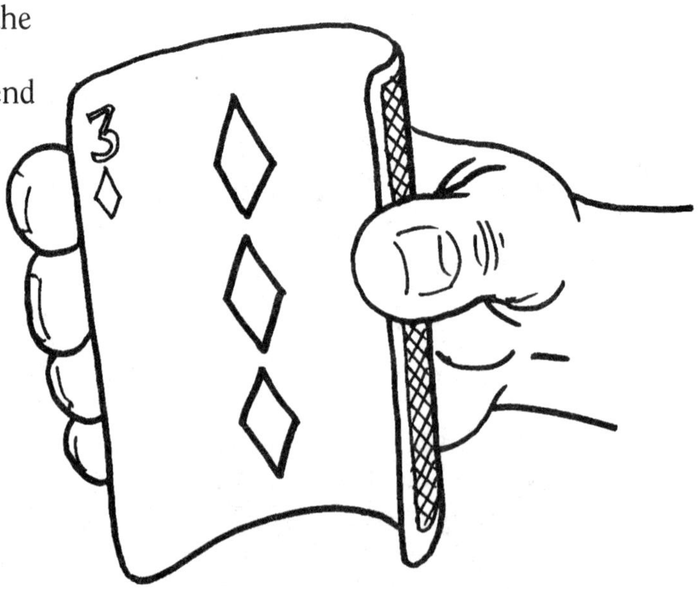

122 SEEK 'N' STEAL

All you have to do is ask the right questions and winning this game will be a real steal!

WHAT YOU'LL NEED

• three to six players

HOW TO PLAY

1. Choose one person to be the dealer. The dealer shuffles the cards and deals out the entire deck, one at a time, face down, to the players. (It doesn't matter if a player or two has one card more than the others.)

2. Each player arranges his or her cards in a fan shape, keeping them hidden, and then arranges them according to sets. A set is a group of matching cards, such as three twos or two kings.

3. The object of this game is to collect all four matching cards to make a book. Each player studies his or her hand to see which cards are needed to make a book.

4. The player to the left of the dealer goes first. He or she asks any one of the other players for a card to help complete a book, calling it out by number and suit. For example, if a player has the two of clubs, the two of spades, and the two of hearts, he or she would say, "I'd like the two of diamonds."

5. If the other player has the card, he or she must hand it over. The first player then asks someone else for another card, and continues on until the player asked for a particular card doesn't have it.

6. The next player takes his or her turn, and then the next player. When a player makes a book of four cards, he or she shows it to the others and places it face down on the table.

7. Players continue taking turns around the circle, asking for cards and making books. Once someone runs out of cards in his or her hand, players count up their books. The player who has the most books wins the game—and earns the reputation for being the sneakiest card thief!

123 HIT THE DECK

This fast-moving party game is sure to be a hit at your next get-together!

WHAT YOU'LL NEED

- six to twenty players
- second deck of regular playing cards, jokers removed
- two shoe boxes

HOW TO PLAY

1. Divide the players into two equal teams. If you have an extra person, that person can act as the judge. If you have an equal number of players, ask your mom or dad to fill in as judge.

2. Have one person put a deck of cards into each shoe box and shake the boxes well to mix up all the cards.

3. Place the boxes side by side on the floor against a wall, about two feet away from each other.

4. One team lines up ten feet away in front of one box. The other team lines up ten feet away in front of the other box.

5. When the judge says "go," the first member of each team races for his or her team's shoe box. When players reach the box, they flip through the cards until they find a king *of any suit*. With a king in hand, they must race back to where the team is lined up and place the king on the floor next to their line.

6. As soon as a player slaps a king on the floor, the second person in line races to the box and looks for a queen *of the same suit*. The person then runs back to the line and places the queen next to the king. The next person then runs to the box to find a jack that matches the suit of the king and queen.

7. Play continues until one team has found an entire suit of cards in order from king, queen, jack, and ten, down to three, two, and finally the ace. The first team to find the cards in order wins.

124 MYSTERY OF THE MAGIC SYMBOL

Astonish your friends when you use an ancient magic symbol to help you see through a card.

WHAT YOU'LL NEED

- pen or pencil

HOW TO DO IT

1 Grab a friend or family member to be your audience.

2 Tell your friend, "I've discovered an ancient symbol that gives me X-ray vision. If I write down the symbol on the face of a card, I will have X-ray vision and be able to see through the card."

3 To demonstrate, hold the deck in the hand you do not write with. Turn the top card face up and place it on top of the deck, about ½ inch lower than the deck.

4 Draw a symbol of your choice in the middle of the face of the card with a pen or pencil. Afterward, quickly place a tiny dot on the top border of the back of the card behind the card you have drawn the symbol on. Make sure no one sees you draw the dot. Your friend will think that the symbol itself will help you find this marked card. But in reality, you'll use the dot to find the card.

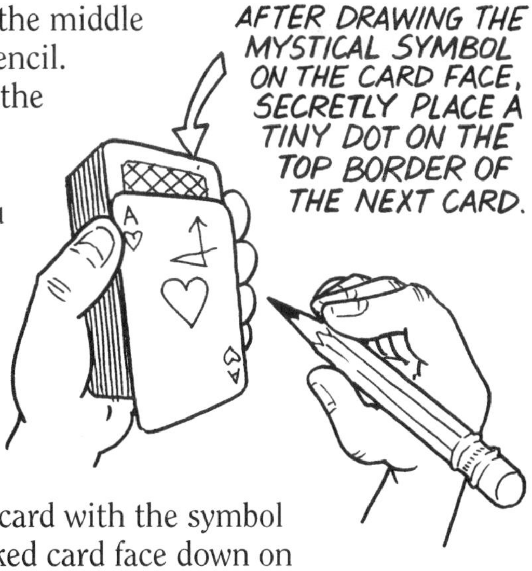

5 Push up the top card so it is no longer lower than the rest of the deck. This will hide the dot. Hold the card with the symbol out to your friend. Now turn the marked card face down on top of the deck. Hand the deck to your friend.

6 Tell your friend to deal off about half the deck, one card at a time, into a heap on the table. He or she will bury the marked card on the bottom. Take back the remaining deck and place the heap of cards on top.

7 Slowly turn over one card at a time into a pile. When you get to the card with the dot on the back of the card, stop as if you're concentrating for a second, then turn over the card. Tell your friend, "I am able to see through this next card. It is the card with the symbol."

8 Turn the card over and hand the card with the symbol to your friend. He or she will be amazed by your incredible X-ray vision!

125 GO BOOM!

In this tension-packed game, you try to get rid of all your cards as quickly as possible. It's so exciting, you'll feel like you're sitting on a time bomb that's about to go off.

WHAT YOU'LL NEED

- two to four players
- pen and paper for scoring

HOW TO PLAY

1 Choose one person to be the dealer. The dealer hands out seven cards to each player, one at a time, face down. The dealer places the leftover cards in the middle, called the stockpile.

2 Players arrange their cards in a fan shape, keeping others from seeing their hand. The player to the left of the dealer goes first by taking any card from his or her hand and laying it next to the stockpile, face up. This is the "lead card."

3 If the second player has a card that matches either the number or suit of the lead card, he or she lays it down next to the lead card. If not, he or she must draw cards from the stockpile until a match is made.

4 Each player takes a turn making a match. Once everyone has laid out a card, look at the cards that have been played. The person who played the highest card in the *suit* of the lead card has to pick up the stack of cards and add them to his or her hand.

5 The second player now lays down a new lead card. Again, everyone puts down a card in either the same suit or number as the lead card.

6 Continue playing. The first player to get rid of all of his or her cards yells "BOOM!" and is the winner. If you want to keep score, players who still have cards should add up the points left in their hand. The points are:

aces.. 1
kings, queens, jacks 10
all other cards............................numeric value

The person with the lowest total score wins.

126 GOSSIP

If you need an icebreaker for your next party, try this game and you'll have everyone instantly knowing everyone else.

WHAT YOU'LL NEED

- ten to eighteen players

HOW TO PLAY

❶ Remove the numbered cards in the suits of hearts and diamonds. You should have a matching pair of hearts and diamonds cards with the same value for every two players. If you have an odd number of guests, you should play. Otherwise, you need to sit out this game. Set all the other cards aside.

❷ Mix up the deck, then as the guests come to the door, give each one a card.

❸ Tell each guest to find his or her partner, the person with the matching card. For example, the guest with the six of hearts is the partner of the person who has the six of diamonds.

❹ Once partners meet, they must share things they love or things they wish for, based on the number and suit of their cards. For instance, a player who has the ten of hearts must tell ten things he or she loves, while a player who has four of diamonds tells his or her four wishes.

❺ Gather in a group, and starting with the highest card, the ten, ask each player to stand up and remember at least one thing his or her partner loves or wishes for. Once everyone has shared, take up the cards, hand them out, and play another round with different partners.

ONE STEP FURTHER: You can also play this game with spades (players say things they don't like) and clubs (players list their favorite places to visit).

127 THE TELLTALE TELEPHONE

With this trick that uses a telephone, you may be a phone-y, but your pals will never know it.

WHAT YOU'LL NEED

- friend at another telephone
- your own telephone

HOW TO DO IT

1. First arrange for a friend to phone you at a certain time. Tell this friend to let the phone ring twice, then hang up, call right back and let the phone ring three times, and then hang up for good.

2. About ten minutes before the time scheduled for the call, grab some friends or family members to be your audience. Tell your audience, "In this trick, one of you will choose a card and not show it to me. I am going to use the help of a psychic friend to help me find the card. She (or he) will call on the telephone, and the number of times my friend rings will tell me exactly where your card is."

3. Choose a person in your audience to shuffle the deck. Tell him or her to take off fifteen cards from the top and place them in a pocket or to the side, because you won't be needing them. This trick can only work using thirty-seven cards.

4. Next, tell the person to count off fifteen more cards from the top. Ask the friend to look at and remember the fifteenth card. He or she then replaces the fifteen cards on top of the deck, keeping them in the same order.

5. Ask your friend to begin turning cards over and reading them off, from the top of the deck. After reading each card, he or she is to place each face down on the bottom of the deck. Pretend that you are listening for a certain card. Actually, you are counting the cards being turned over. When your friend turns over the twenty-ninth card, say, "Wait. I'm getting vibes from my friend. She's going to call any minute and tell me which card you selected."

❻ If you have to kill some time before your friend calls, fill up the time by saying something like, "My psychic friend has never failed to correctly identify a card."

❼ Continue talking until the phone rings. It will ring twice, then three times. Turn to your audience and say, "Two rings and three rings. That means the card you chose is the twenty-third card from the top of the deck."

❽ Ask the person holding the cards to turn over twenty-three cards. The twenty-third card will be the card he or she chose in the beginning! Your psychic friend was right again!

THE SECRET TO THE TRICK: It's based on a mathematical formula that works due to the number of cards you use (only thirty-seven) and the number of cards you have your friend count off (twenty-nine, then twenty-three). The use of a psychic telephone friend is just a fun way to display the trick.

128 TWENTY-TWO

Now matter how you count it, this game adds up to a lot of fun—and sometimes even more than one winner.

WHAT YOU'LL NEED

- two to eight players

HOW TO PLAY

1 Choose one person to be the dealer. The dealer shuffles the cards and deals one card to each player, face down. Next, the dealer passes out a second card to each player, face up.

2 The object of the game is to have two cards whose point value is as close to twenty-two without going over twenty-two. The points for cards are: aces can be either two points or twelve points (the choice is up to the player); face cards are ten points; and points for all the other cards are the number on the card.

3 Players study their cards and add up their numbers.

4 The dealer asks the person on the left if that player wants another card. If the player's point total is close to twenty-two, he or she should say, "Stay," which means he or she doesn't want another card. If the player's point total is low, he or she should say, "Hit," which means he or she wants another card.

5 After being "hit" with one card, the player can ask for as many hits as he or she wants. But remember: You don't want to have a point total over twenty-two!

6 The dealer goes around the circle, asking each player if he or she wants more cards.

7 Once everyone has had a turn, players turn their cards face up. The person who has a point total closest to twenty-two without going over is the winner! If more than one player shares the same winning point total, they're all winners.

129 THE RISING CARD

PARENTAL SUPERVISION REQUIRED

You'll get a rise out of your friends when you actually lift cards magically out of the box!

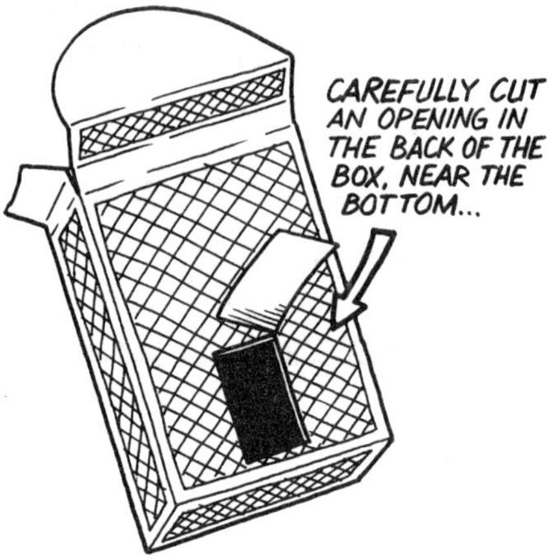

WHAT YOU'LL NEED

- pencil or pen
- scissors
- cardboard box the cards came in

HOW TO DO IT

1 Before you present this trick, you have to prepare the box. Remove the cards from the box. Use the pencil or pen to draw a small square, about ½ inch by ½ inch, on the back of the card box, near the bottom. Ask your parents to use the scissors to carefully cut this square out and throw it away.

2 Replace the cards in the box. Grab a pal to be your audience. To begin the trick, open the box and slide out the cards. Show the cards to your audience, saying, "This is just a normal deck of playing cards. But I can control them whenever I want." Slip the cards back into the box.

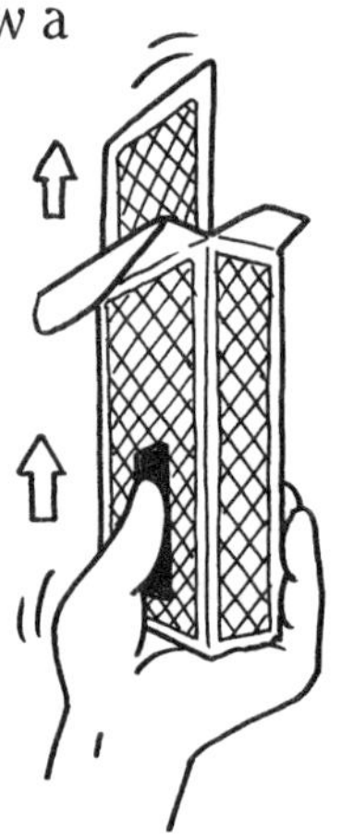

3 Hold the box vertically in your left hand with the hole in the back facing you. Keep your fingers on the front of the box and your thumb on the back. Wave your right hand over the box and say a few magic words, such as "presto, change-o." While you are talking, put your thumb over the hole in the box. You will be touching the first card inside. Work your thumb up and down, pressing through the hole. This will slide up the card inside the box, until it sticks out from the top of the box. Abra-card-abra! The card moved without you seeming to touch it!

130 CRAZY ACES

You'd be crazy to pass up playing this old favorite with a new twist!

WHAT YOU'LL NEED

• two to four players

HOW TO PLAY

1 Choose one person to be the dealer. The dealer shuffles and passes out seven cards, one at a time, face down to each player. The dealer then places the leftover cards in the middle, face down. This is called the pickup pile. The dealer turns the top card on the pickup pile face up to start a second pile. This is called the throw-away pile.

2 Players arrange their cards into a fan shape and group the cards according to suit. They also separate out all of the aces and put them together.

3 The object of this game is for each player to match the top card on the throw-away pile with a card from his or her hand. Players can either match the suit or the number of the card. For example, if the top card of the throw-away pile is the five of spades, any spade card or a five in another suit matches. If another five is played, the suit now changes to that of the new card. All four aces are wild. This means you can play an ace on top of any card and choose the suit you want it to be. If a player can't match the suit OR number of the card, he or she must draw from the pick-up pile until he or she finds a card to play.

4 The player to the left of the dealer goes first, finding a card that matches the card on the throw-away pile. Players take turns around the circle.

5 When the pickup pile runs out, the dealer shuffles the throw-away pile and turns it face down to make a new pickup pile. The first person to get rid of all the cards in his or her hand is the winner.

131 DUNK IN THE OCEAN

Dip into this entertaining game where the object is to get rid of your cards as quickly as possible. You and your friends are sure to get along swimmingly!

WHAT YOU'LL NEED

- two to seven players
- regular deck of playing cards for *each* player

HOW TO PLAY

1. Each player shuffles his or her own deck of cards. Each player then lays out five stacks of seven cards face up in front of him or her. Each person sets the leftover cards, the "dunk pile," aside.

2. Together, players say "dunk," and in unison turn up one card from their dunk piles and place them in the center playing area.

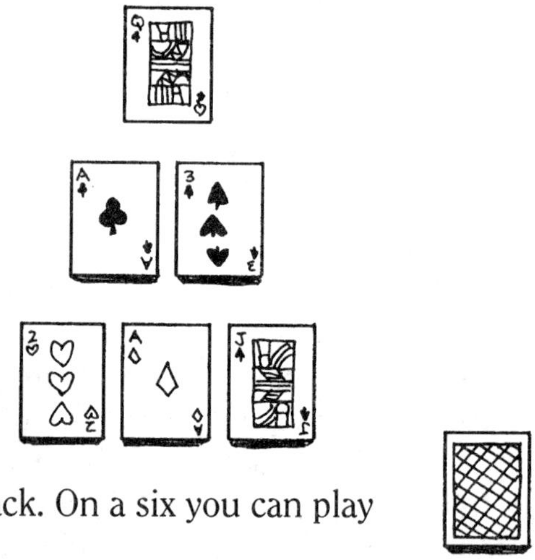

3. Players then check the top cards of their five stacks to see if any of them can be played on any of the cards in the middle. Players can play a card in any suit that is either higher or lower than the card in the middle. For example, on a queen you can play either a king or a jack. On a six you can play either a seven or a five.

4. Players rapidly play as many cards as they can from their stacks.

5. When there are no more cards that can be played, players say "dunk" again and in unison turn up new cards from their dunk piles and place them on top of the cards in the center.

6. Continue playing until one person has played off all of the cards in his or her five stacks. The first person to get rid of his or her cards wins!

132 WHAT A CARD!

You'll stand out from the pack when you make your own deck of playing cards, personalized with your favorite designs and photos.

WHAT YOU'LL NEED

- pencil
- scissors
- glue
- ruler
- large sheet of light-colored construction paper or lightweight cardboard, 22 inches by 28 inches
- stickers—thirteen stickers each of four different symbols (or suits) like rainbows, stars, suns, and clouds (about 2 inches in diameter)
- back design—fifty-two copies of the same design
- marking pens in two to four complementary colors

HOW TO DO IT

1 Using the pencil and ruler, begin by marking a small dot every 2½ inches along both of the *long* edges of the construction paper or cardboard.

2 Next, mark small dots every 3½ inches along both *short* edges of the construction paper. Use the ruler to connect the dots, vertically and horizontally, with a light pencil line. You need at least fifty-two 2½-inch-by-3½-inch rectangles. These pencil lines will be your cutting lines. But don't cut yet.

3 Decide on the back design. If you are using a photograph, you can have it photocopied at a copying facility. Make sure the photo will fit inside the 3½-inch-by-2½-inch card. (To save money on photocopying, make ten copies first. Cut and paste or tape all ten photos to one sheet of paper, then copy that paper five times.)

4 Once you have your fifty-two back designs, glue them inside the penciled rectangles on your sheet. Let glue dry for several hours.

5 Once glue is dry, carefully cut along the pencil lines until you have your fifty-two-card deck. One side will bear your design; the other side should be blank.

6 Separate the cards into four piles of thirteen cards each. Make sure the cards are arranged with all the tops pointing the same way.

7 Now flip the stacks over to show the blank sides of the cards. You are now going to create your suits. Choose one sticker design for each suit and apply one sticker to the middle of each card. Choose two colors of marking pens and begin marking your cards in the upper left-hand corner in the following order: king, queen, jack, ten, nine, eight, seven, six, five, four, three, two, and ace. Turn the cards face down and keep in order after marking. Color two suits in one color and two suits in a different color.

8 Flip the stack over and turn the cards around so that the numbers or letters are on the right-hand side of the cards and appear upside down. Using the same color marking pens, repeat and mark the top left-hand side of the cards exactly as before. When you're finished, you'll have your own deck of personalized cards!

TO MAKE IT TOUGHER: To make your cards last longer, you have the option of having them laminated. Most copying facilities can laminate for a small charge. If you plan to laminate, it is best to design and decorate *both* the front and back of your cards *before* cutting. This way you can have the whole sheet laminated at one time, which is easier and cheaper. (Mark your pencil cutting lines on *both* sides of the paper before decorating. This will ensure that your designs stay within the lines.)

133 TRADING PLACES

Your friends will jump at the chance to find out how you make two cards, the eight of hearts and the seven of diamonds, jump from the bottom of the deck to the top.

HOW TO DO IT

❶ Before you demonstrate this trick, pull out four cards—eight of hearts, eight of diamonds, seven of hearts, and seven of diamonds—when no one is looking. Place the eight of hearts and the seven of diamonds on the top of the stack. Put the eight of diamonds and the seven of hearts aside.

❷ Grab a few friends to be your audience. Show the eight of diamonds and the seven of hearts to your audience to prove to them that they're normal cards.

❸ Ask someone to place these two cards on the bottom of the deck. Next, tell your audience that you're going to magically make these two cards appear on the top of the deck.

❹ Quickly knock three times on the top of the deck and turn up the top two cards. These cards are actually the eight of *hearts* and seven of *diamonds*, which you put there earlier, but your audience will think they're the eight of diamonds and the seven of hearts that were placed on the bottom of the deck. Most people will never notice the switch because the cards look so much alike!

134 MY SHIP SAILS

All on board! This is one card game that will suit anyone—as long as the player collects enough cards of one suit!

WHAT YOU'LL NEED

• three or more players

HOW TO PLAY

1. Choose one person to be the dealer. The dealer shuffles the cards and deals out seven cards, one at a time, face down, to each player. The dealer sets the leftover cards aside.

2. Players pick up their cards and arrange them in a fan shape.

3. The goal of the game is to collect seven cards of the same suit. When the dealer says "go," players in unison take one card they don't want from their hands, lay it face down on the table or floor, and slide it to the player on their left.

4. Players pick up their new cards and put them in their hands, then each chooses another card to pass. Players continue passing cards around the table until one person has all seven cards in the same suit. This person says, "My ship sails!" and lays down his or her cards to show the rest of the players that the game is over!

135 ALL IN THE SHUFFLE

This trick is based on a complicated mathematical formula. But it's a breeze to perform, because your audience does all the work!

HOW TO DO IT

1 Tell a friend, "You have the power to be a magician, and I can prove it. In this trick, you will remove one card, bury it in a stack of cards, then find it again!"

2 Next, take ten cards off the top of a deck and give them to your friend. Set the rest of the cards aside—you won't be using them. Tell the friend to shuffle the ten cards and then choose one card, but not to tell you what it is.

3 Tell your friend to count the number of cards from the top of the stack to, and including, the chosen card and remember this number.

4 Take the cards from your friend, saying, "I will cut the deck exactly in half." Push off the top five cards and move them to the bottom. Hand the cards back to your friend.

5 Ask your friend what number he or she remembered from Step 3. Then ask him or her to move that number of cards, one at a time, from the top of the stack to the bottom.

TO PERFORM THE ELIMINATION SHUFFLE, SIMPLY TAKE THE TOP CARD AND PUT IT ON THE BOTTOM--

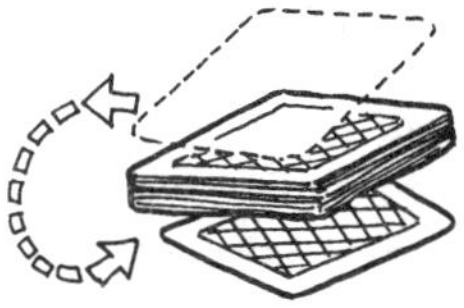

--THEN TAKE THE NEXT CARD AND PLACE IT ON THE TABLE...

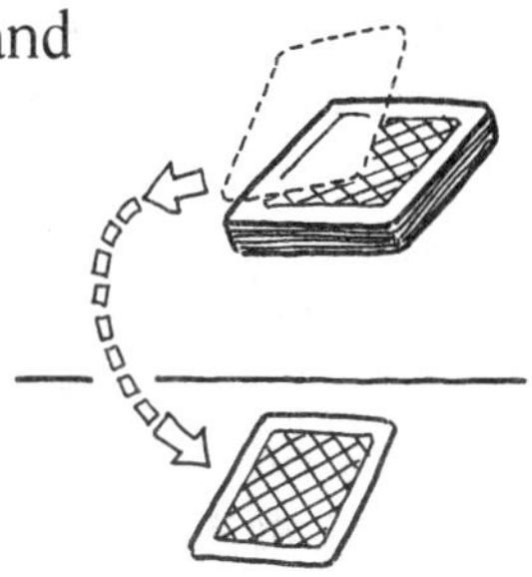

...REPEAT THIS PROCESS UNTIL ONLY ONE CARD IS LEFT IN YOUR HAND.

6 Now ask your friend to perform the "elimination shuffle," and that this will magically reveal his or her chosen card. To do the elimination shuffle, have your friend take the top card and put it at the bottom of the deck. Then take the next card and put it on a table. Take the following card and put it on the bottom of the deck. The next card is placed on the table, and so on.

7 The friend continues the elimination shuffle until only one card is left. Ask your friend to turn over that last card. Guess what? It will be his or her chosen card!

136 ON THE NOSE

The players who win this game will stand out as plain as the noses on their faces!

WHAT YOU'LL NEED

- four to thirteen players

HOW TO PLAY

1. Depending on the number of players, you first need to figure out how many cards will be used. With four players you use only the aces, kings, queens, and jacks. The rest of the cards are set aside. With five players, add the tens. With six players, add the nines; with seven players, add the eights; with eight players, add the sevens; and so on.

2. Choose one person to be the dealer. The dealer shuffles the cards and hands them all out, one at a time, face down, to the players.

3. Players arrange the cards in a fan shape, then by sets. A set is a group of matching cards, such as three jacks or two nines. The object of this game is to collect a book—four cards that match.

4. When the dealer says "go," each player takes a card out of his or her hand and passes it to the player on his or her left. Players add the new cards to their hands, arranging them by number.

5. Continue playing until one person has a book. The first person to collect a book quietly lays a finger on his or her nose. As soon as the other players notice the finger, they should quickly and quietly touch their noses, too. The last person to touch his or her nose is the loser.

STRATEGY ALERT: Don't discard two or more matching cards. Hold onto those cards and try to make a book.

137

WHAT AN ACE!

You'll look oh so impressive when you find an ace without even looking at the deck of cards.

WHAT YOU'LL NEED

- table that you and your friend can reach under

HOW TO DO IT

1. Sit across the table from your friend. While you shuffle the deck of cards, take a peek at the card on the bottom and remember it.

2. Hand the deck, face down, to your friend. Ask your friend to turn the cards face up, fan through them, and find an ace—any ace. Ask the friend to then turn the deck face down again, and place the ace on top of the deck. Also ask him or her to take a look at the bottom card, and to remember it.

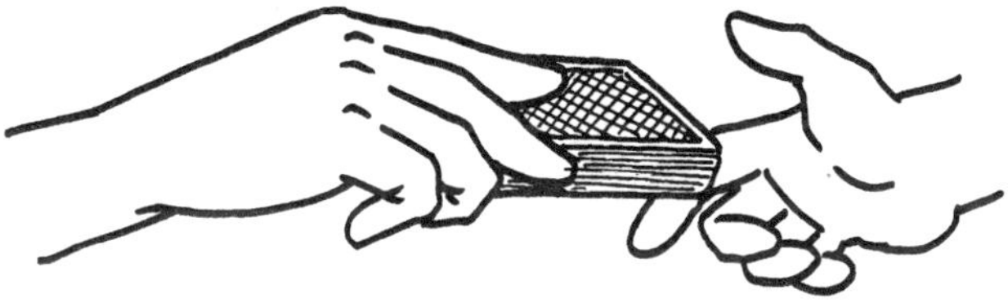

3. When your friend is finished, ask him or her to hand you the deck under the table. Grab the deck with your right hand and turn your palm over so the deck is now face up. This reverses the order of the cards. Now the ace is on the bottom.

AFTER YOU GRAB THE DECK, TURN YOUR PALM OVER SO THE DECK IS FACE UP...

4. Tell your friend to reach under the table and take the top card. Ask that his or her hands stay *under* the table the whole time. Your friend will think the card is the ace that he or she put on top. But since you turned the cards over, he or she will really be taking the *bottom* card.

5. Both of you keep your hands under the table. Next, tell your friend to place the "ace" into the middle of the deck.

6 Secretly turn your hand over so that the ace is now back on top.

7 Still keep your hands under the table. Ask your friend to take the bottom card off the deck and hand it to you under the table. Say, "This card will help me find your ace." Keep one hand with the cards under the table. Bring the bottom card out and look at it. Say the name of the card you remember seeing on the bottom, out loud. This will *not* be the card you are looking at. Put this card back under the table and onto the bottom of the deck.

8 Rap the bottom of the table with your hand three times. Take the top card off the deck and bring it up to the table. Turn it over and show that it is your friend's ace. Because your friend thought he or she hid the ace in the middle of the deck, your friend will be very impressed that you found it!

9 For the finish, hand your friend the deck of cards and tell him or her to find the original bottom card. Your friend will be amazed to find this card is now in the middle of the deck.

STRATEGY ALERT: The secret to this trick is to remember at all times which way the cards are facing—up or down—while they are under the table.

138 MEMORY MADNESS

This matching game will not only maximize your memory skills but your fun as well!

WHAT YOU'LL NEED

- two to six players

HOW TO PLAY

1 Choose one person to be the dealer. The dealer pulls a card from the middle of the stack and shows it to all the players. This card, and the others with the same value, are wild cards. This means that they will match with any other card.

2 The dealer next lays all the cards, face down, in front of the other players. He or she can lay the cards out in any design he or she wants.

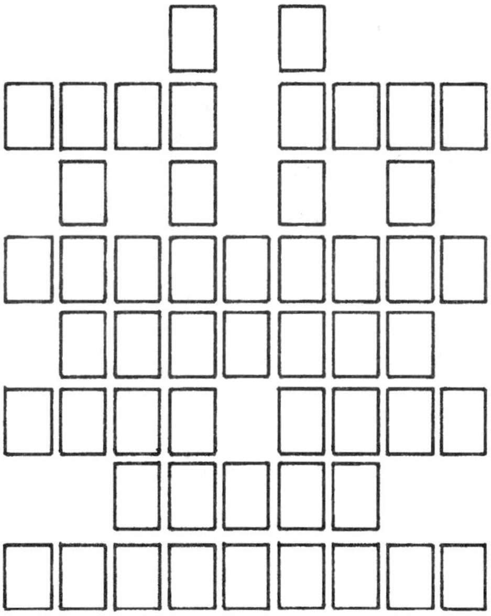

3 The person to the left of the dealer goes first. He or she turns up any two cards. If they make a pair, the player gets to keep them. The player then gets to try to make another match. If the cards don't make a pair, he or she puts them back, turning them face down. The turn goes to the next player.

4 Keep taking turns until all the cards have been paired up. And don't forget the wild card. If it turns up with any other card, it is an automatic match! The player with the most pairs is the winner—and has the most impressive memory!

139 POOF, IT'S GONE!

Where, oh, where did the card go? This is one trick your friends will never figure out—unless you come clean with the secret!

WHAT YOU'LL NEED

- bar of soap

HOW TO DO IT

1. Before you perform this trick, rub a pea-sized dab of soap on the tip of your thumb.

2. Line up your audience on the other side of a small table. Allow one person to shuffle the deck of cards and return it to you.

3. Pick up the top card. Hold it so that your thumb is in the center of the face of the card. While showing it to your audience, rub the dab of soap onto the center of the card.

4. Lay this card face down on the top of the deck and make all the edges even. Tell your audience that you are going to press this card into the middle of the deck and make it disappear. Press hard on top of the deck. (This sets the dab of soap, causing the top two cards to stick together.)

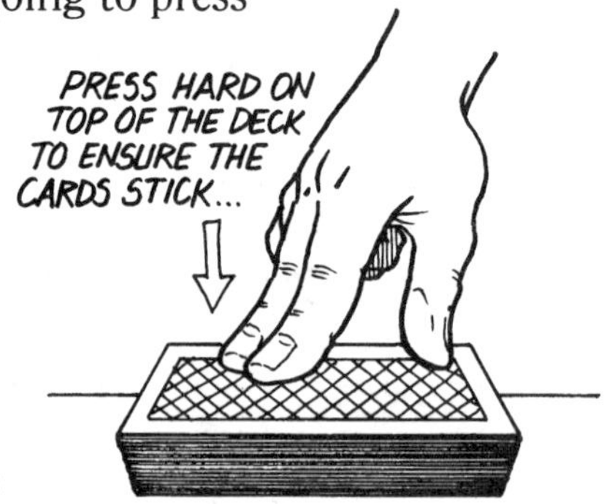

5. Pick up the top card and show it to the audience. This will be a different card than the one you started with because the top card is now stuck to the second card! No one will ever guess your secret!

140

BULL'S EYE

Gather up a group and see who's the best shot.

WHAT YOU'LL NEED

- two to thirteen players
- large hat
- ruler

HOW TO PLAY

1. Give each player four cards that match. For example, one player gets four sevens, another player gets four twos, the next player gets four tens, and so on.

2. Arrange everyone around the room in a giant circle. Place the hat in the middle of the circle.

3. Go around the circle, giving everyone a chance to flip his or her cards into the hat.

4. Use the ruler to measure how close each toss is to the hat. Award players the following points:

more than 12 inches from the hat	0 points
under 12 inches, more than 6 inches	5 points
under 6 inches, more than 2 inches	10 points
under 2 inches	15 points
Bull's-eye	25 points

Add up the points and give a prize—maybe a new hat—to the player with the highest score.

141

KING'S COURT

Your friends will be amazed at your power to place four kings randomly into a deck of cards and then bring them together.

HOW TO DO IT

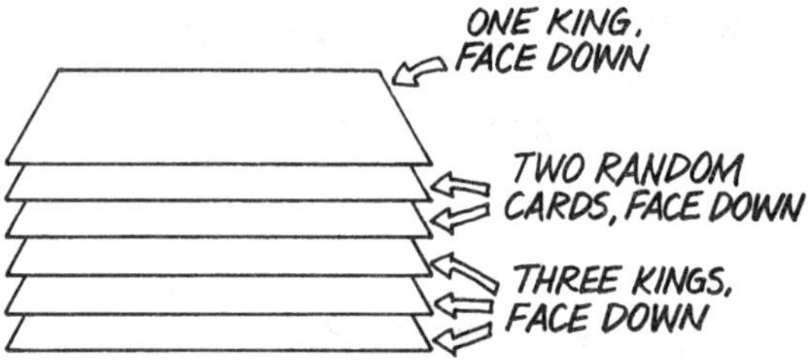

❶ Before performing the trick you need to arrange the cards in a certain order when no one is looking. First, remove the four kings from the deck and set the rest of the deck aside—you'll use it later. Place three kings face down on the table on top of each other. Place *any* two other cards face down on top of the kings. Then place the fourth king on the top, face down. Fan the kings face up so that the two extra cards in the middle are hidden from the audience.

❷ Now that your kings are arranged, call in your audience. Show the four kings to the audience. Next say, "Now I'm going to place three of these kings randomly into the deck." Put your "kings" selection on top of the deck, face down.

❸ Pick up the top card (a king) and place it on the very bottom of the deck. Pick up the second card (not a king) and place it anywhere in the lower half of the deck. Pick up the third card (not a king) and place it anywhere in the upper half of the deck. Now there will be one king on the bottom and three still on top.

❹ Pick up the top half of the cards and set it to your right. Then pick up the bottom half of the cards and place it on top of the stack. The four kings are now together in the middle of the deck.

❺ Now tell your audience, "I will bring the kings back together." Tap gently four times on the deck. Turn the deck face up and fan through the cards until you find all four kings, lined up together, in the middle of the deck. How did you do it? As long as the kings don't talk, your friends will never know!

142 TWO-PERSON RUMMY

This game is one long run to the finish to see which player is the first to have a hand filled with all sets or runs.

WHAT YOU'LL NEED

- two players
- pen or pencil
- paper to keep score on

HOW TO PLAY

1 Choose one person to be the dealer. The dealer shuffles the cards and deals each player ten cards, one at a time, face down. The dealer places the leftover cards face down in the middle of the circle. This is the pickup pile. The dealer turns up the top card on the pickup pile and sets it down, face up, to create a second pile. This is the throw-away pile.

2 Players arrange their hands in a fan shape. Then they arrange their hands in runs or sets. A run is a series of three or more cards in the same suit in numerical order, such as the five, six, and seven of diamonds. A set is three or four cards that are the same number, such as four nines. The first player to have his or her hand filled completely with runs or sets "goes out" and wins the game.

3 The player who didn't deal goes first and gets a chance to choose a new card to help complete a run or set. He or she has the choice of taking a card from the pickup pile or from the throw-away pile. After picking up the new card, the player discards a card from his or her hand onto the throw-away pile, face up.

❹ The second player then chooses and discards a card. Players take turns until one player's hand is filled with all the cards in sets or runs. The winning player discards the final card face down on the throw-away pile, then lays down all of the cards, displaying the runs and sets. This is called "rummy."

❺ The first person to rummy gets points from the other player's cards. Any cards that do not make up a complete run or a complete set will count as points. The points are:

aces..11 points
kings, queens, jacks ....10 points
all other cards ....numeric value

❻ Add up all the points and keep score. Play as many games as you can or until one person makes 100 points. The first person to get 100 points is the grand winner!

TO MAKE IT TOUGHER: Alternate games. In one game, make only runs allowable. In the next game, make only sets allowable.

143 BLIND MAN'S POKER

In this goofy game you get to look at your opponent's card and NOT your own!

WHAT YOU'LL NEED

- two players
- pen and paper for keeping score

HOW TO PLAY

1 Players sit across from each other. One person is the dealer. He or she shuffles the cards and deals out one card to each player, face down. Players do not look at their cards.

2 When the dealer says "go," both players pick up their cards at the same time and hold them to their foreheads, face out, toward the other player. Now they can see the other player's card but not their own.

3 The player who is not the dealer goes first and guesses if his or her card is higher than the other person's card. Then the second player makes a guess as to whose card is higher.

4 Both players then lay their cards down and see if they were right.

5 Each player gets 10 points for a correct guess, plus the points of their card. The points for cards are:

aces ....15 points
kings, queens, jacks ....10 points
all other cards...numeric value

After the first round, the next person deals.

6 Keep playing until one person wins 100 points.

144

CLASH

This variation of the game of War makes for a fun face-off with a friend.

WHAT YOU'LL NEED

- two players

HOW TO PLAY

❶ Choose one person to be the dealer. The dealer draws one card out of the middle of the stack and shows it to the other player. This card and the others with the same value—for example, all sixes or all jacks—will be wild for this game. The wild card beats any other card.

❷ The dealer shuffles the cards and deals out the entire deck, one at a time, face down, into two stacks, one stack for each player. Players pick up their stacks, but do not look at them.

❸ Both players turn up their top cards at the same time in the middle of the playing area. The person with the highest card wins both the cards—unless it's a wild card, which is the automatic winner. The player with the high card collects the cards in the middle and places them, face down, under his or her stack.

❹ Players continue turning over cards and winning sets of cards.

❺ The real fun comes when players turn over cards that match, such as two tens or two queens. This is the "clash" you've been waiting for. To settle the dispute, both players place three cards, face down, next to their clash card. Then both players turn up a fourth card. The person with the highest fourth card wins all the cards in the middle. (And if the two cards turned over at this point match, place three more cards face down and face off again!)

❻ Keep playing until one person has all the cards. Or, if you're exhausted from battle and want to end the game early, count up your cards. The person with the most cards is the winner.

TO MAKE IT TOUGHER: After three "clashes" in one game, the dealer can pick another wild card from an extra deck of cards so there are two types of wild cards to look out for.

145 SIX AND THREE-QUARTERS

This cute magic trick will not only wow your audience, it also comes with a built-in play on words.

WHAT YOU'LL NEED

- deck of cards with jokers

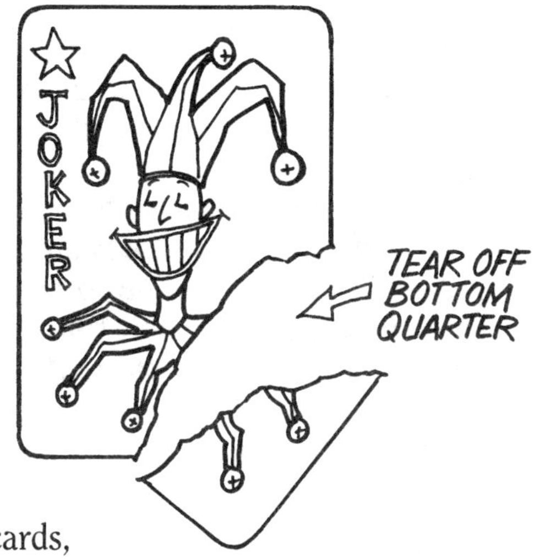

HOW TO DO IT

1 First, you'll need to prepare the deck when no one is looking. To start, pull out the two of clubs and set it aside. Then, tear off the bottom quarter of the joker. Place this joker on the table, face down. Count any six cards from the top of the deck, face down, and cover the joker. Finally, place the two of clubs on top of the six cards, face up. Place the rest of the deck face down on top of the two of clubs. Now you're ready to perform the trick.

2 Grab a friend to be your audience. Fan the cards out in front of your friend and ask him or her to select a card from the middle of the deck, remember it, then replace it on top of the deck, face down. Tell your friend, "Now I am going to find your card."

3 Take the cards and cut them. This puts the chosen card underneath your joker, which will help you find it. Tell your friend that first you are going to look for the two of clubs, because it will help you find the card he or she selected.

4 Flip through the cards until you come to the two of clubs, which is easy to find because it is face up. While you show this card to your friend, move the cards that came before the two of clubs to the bottom of the deck face down. Lay the two of clubs aside—you don't need it anymore.

5 Now you're ready to find the card—and make a play on words at the same time—based on the way you've set up the deck. Tell your friend, "According to my calculations, your card is exactly six and three-quarters down from the top!"

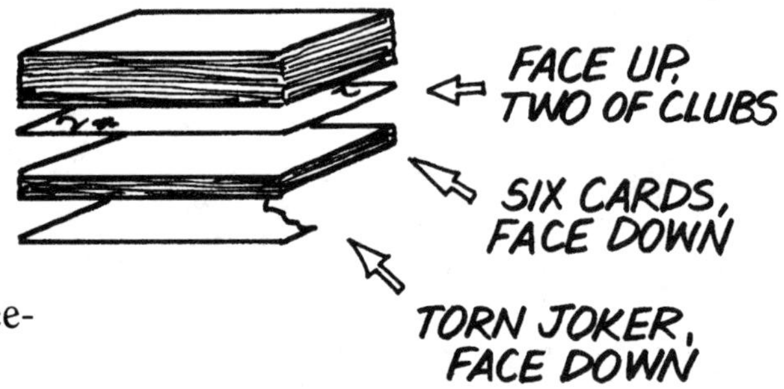

6 Your friend won't know what you mean yet, but that's okay. Slowly, dramatically deal cards off the top, counting as you go: "One . . . two . . ." and so on, until you count six. The next card is the joker. Pick it up and show that it is only three-quarters of a card, then say, ". . . and three-quarters. That means your card is right here!"

7 Pick up the next card on the stack, turning it up to show it is the card he or she picked at the very beginning!

146 BOWLING SOLITAIRE

You don't need to go to the bowling alley to play this game that will really knock you over!

HOW TO PLAY

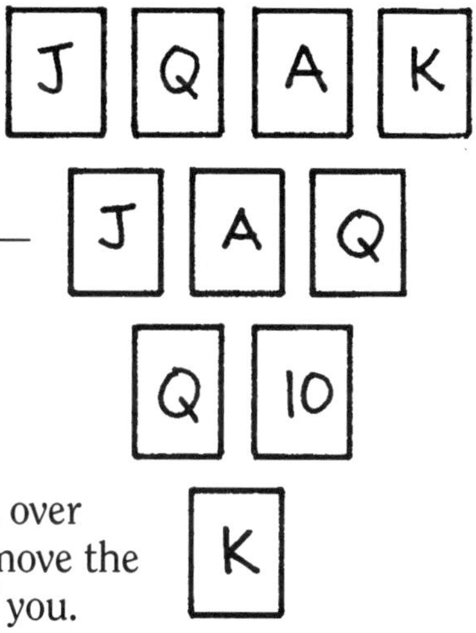

1 Remove all the aces, kings, queens, jacks, and tens from the deck. This will give you twenty cards. Set the rest of the deck aside—you won't be needing it.

2 Shuffle the twenty cards and then lay out the first ten, *face up*, in bowling pin layout.

3 The other cards are your "ball" cards. Turn over a ball card. If it matches a bowling pin card, remove the pin card from the layout and place it in front of you.

4 Keep turning over ball cards and removing pin cards. If you remove all the pin cards before you run out of ball cards, you win.

147 ABOUT FACE

This easy but entertaining trick works due to the fact that the deck mixes both face-up and face-down cards.

HOW TO DO IT

1. Give a friend a deck of cards and ask him or her to cut the cards into three nearly equal piles. The exact number of cards in each pile doesn't matter.

2. Next, ask your friend to pick up one pile and shuffle it. Then ask him or her to look at the top card on this pile and remember it.

3. Ask your friend to place this pile FACE UP on top of either of the two FACE-DOWN piles. The remaining pile should be placed FACE DOWN on top of this stack. The deck will now have both FACE-UP and FACE-DOWN cards.

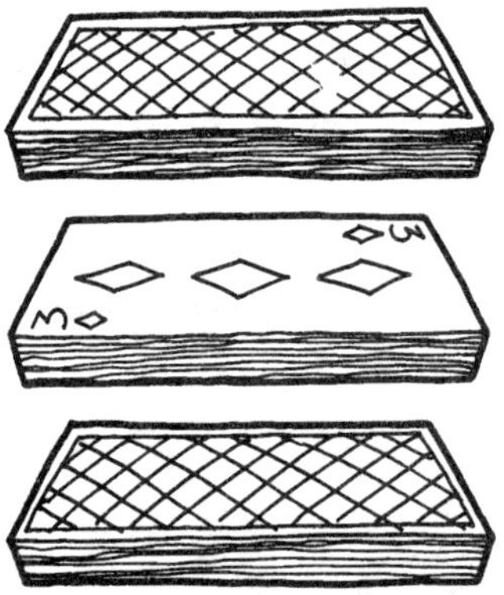

4. For the next step, ask your friend to cut the deck, shuffle the cards, then give you back the deck. Say, "Now I will find the card you chose."

5. Turn the deck FACE UP and fan through the cards until you come to the first long string of FACE-UP cards. Fan past these cards to the very next FACE-DOWN card. Turn this card up, and it will be the card your friend noted in the beginning.

148 DON'T LOOK BACK!

This trick is so simple, you can find a chosen card with both hands behind your back. The challenge is fooling your audience into thinking the trick is harder than it really is!

HOW TO DO IT

1 Fan out the deck of cards and offer them, face down, to someone in your audience. Ask him or her to pick a card and not to let you see what it is.

2 Put the cards back into a single deck and ask that person to place the chosen card on the bottom of the deck.

3 Take the cards behind your back and tell your audience that you're going to find the selected card by mixing up the cards. But instead of mixing up the cards, slide the bottom card around to the top of the deck and turn it over so that it is face up.

WHILE THE DECK IS BEHIND YOUR BACK, SLIDE THE CHOSEN CARD AROUND FROM BOTTOM TO THE TOP.

4 After a few seconds, bring the deck around to the front. Hold the deck in front of you so that the *bottom* card points toward your audience. The card facing you (on top) is the card your friend picked. Remember it.

5 The hard part of the trick is over for you, because you already know which card your friend selected. The rest of the trick is to fool your audience into thinking that the trick is a lot harder than it actually is, so they'll be more impressed with your magic skills. To do this, ask the audience if the bottom card you're showing is the chosen card. The audience will groan and say no. You can reply, "Just kidding, folks!"

6 Next, tell your audience that you're going to mix up the cards behind your back one more time and try again to find the chosen card. But instead of mixing up the cards, turn the selected card over so the back is showing like the others, and slide it back into the deck.

7 Bring the deck around to the front. Tell your audience that you're going to look for the chosen card. Begin to turn over cards, studying each one for a second as if it might be the chosen card.

8 While you are turning over cards, you will pass the chosen card. Don't let on that you know it's the chosen card—keep the suspense building for a few more minutes. Your audience will probably groan or giggle and think you've really blown the trick.

9 Turn over a few more cards, then announce, "The next card I turn over will be the chosen card." Everyone will probably burst out laughing because they know you've already passed the card. With a straight face, reach down into the cards you've already turned over and find the chosen card. Show it to your audience, then turn it over face down and say, "Here it is!" Your audience will be shocked and surprised that you pulled this one off!

149 CAPTURE THE CARD

Be the general of your own army of cards and try to take the most "prisoners" from your opponent's hands.

WHAT YOU'LL NEED

• two players

HOW TO PLAY

1. Players sit across from each other at a table or on the floor.

2. Choose one person to be the dealer. The dealer shuffles the cards and deals them all out, one at a time, face down, in two stacks, one for each player.

3. Players pick up their stacks but don't look at their cards.

4. The player who didn't deal begins the game by turning the top card face up and placing it in the center playing area. The dealer then turns his or her top card face up, and places it head-to-head with the first card.

5. If the cards are number cards (ten, nine, eight, seven, six, five, four, three, or two), each player turns up another card. Continue playing until one person turns over an ace or a face card.

6. The first player to turn up an ace or a face card says, "Prepare to be my prisoner." The second player answers, "Not if I can help it!" He or she then turns up from *one to four cards*, hoping to find an ace or face card higher than the first player's card. If he or she doesn't turn over a higher card, the first player takes all the cards in the center playing area as his or her "prisoners." But, if the second player is lucky and

turns up a higher card, he or she announces, "Now prepare to be *my* prisoner!" The first player is now under attack. He or she can turn over as many as four cards to try to find an even higher card. If he or she can't, the second player wins all the cards in the center playing area. If at any point there is a tie, both players turn over a card, and that highest card determines the winner for that round.

7 Players return to their stacks and begin again, turning up one card at a time. Continue to "battle" for cards each time an ace or face card is turned up. If at any time both players turn up the same card, such as two kings, they each turn up as many cards as it takes until one turns up a higher card.

8 The player who finally runs out of cards loses, and the game is over.

9 If you run out of time and have to stop playing before one person has captured all the cards, have each player count his or her captured cards. The person with the most cards wins the game—and the war!

150

GO FOR IT!

You'll probably get your friends to go for this silly game only once. So get a group together and give it your best shot!

HOW TO PLAY

1. Gather your friends into a circle and tell them, "You are about to play the most incredible, amazing, unbelievable card game in the history of mankind. It's called Go for It."

2. Hold all the cards in one hand and throw them in the air.

3. While your friends look at you, wondering what kind of game this is, tell them, "Go for it."

4. Explain that the trick is that they have to "go for" all the cards and pick them up. You can expect a few grumbles, but most of your pals will no doubt grin and bear it and pick up all the cards.